100 TIPS
for
Drums
you should have been told

Printed in the United Kingdom by MPG Books Ltd, Bodmin

Published by Sanctuary Publishing Limited, Sanctuary House, 45–53 Sinclair Road, London W14 0NS, United Kingdom

www.sanctuarypublishing.com

Music typesetting: Cambridge Notation

Cover photograph: © Getty Images

ISBN: 1-86074-435-4

100 TIPS
for
Drums
you should have been told

PETE RILEY

Sanctuary

ACKNOWLEDGEMENTS

Firstly, I'd like to thank my wife, Joe, and the kids, Ellie and Billy, for putting up with me being around even less than usual. Special thanks should also go to Phil Hilborne for his patience and expertise in piecing the CD together.

There's also an extra-special nod to Mike Sturgis for putting me forward to do this project in the first place, and Chris Francis must get a mention for doing his usual fabulous job of interpreting my scribbles and making it all legible. Thanks also to my teacher, Bob Armstrong, for pointing me in the right direction.

And, finally, I couldn't do any of this without support from the following wonderful people and companies: Colin and George at Premier Drums, Tina and Bob at Zildjian, Jerome at Arbiters/Vic Firth Sticks and Gary at Remo.

This book is dedicated to Bob Armstrong, for showing me the way.

BOOK CONTENTS

CD CONTENTS

All highlighted examples refer to chapter/section headings. All non-highlighted items refer to examples within the given chapter.

Pete used Premier Signia Marquis (maple) drums with 10", 12", 14" and 16" toms and a 22" (or occasionally an 18") bass drum. Snares were either a 5" Signia maple or Ludwig 400. Cymbals were all Zildjian, heads all Remo and mics a combination of Shure and AKG.

CD produced, engineered, recorded and mixed (all illustrative examples) by Pete Riley @ Tindrum Studios. CD compiled, mastered, edited and voiceovers recorded/mixed by Phil Hilborne at WM Studios. Web: www.philhilborne.com. CD copyright: © Pete Riley, 2003.

Email info@peteriley.net. Web: www.peteriley.net.

FOREWORD

Drums are arguably one of the most fun instruments to play. The basics of it are much easier to pick up than, say, guitar (all those chord shapes!) and the piano (is that as loud as it gets?). But what happens after you've learned to play a few basic beats and played along to a few CDs? At this point, budding percussionists usually fall into two categories: those who are happy simply playing the music they like in the way they like, and those who want to learn more about the possibilities of the instrument. I'm guessing that, since you're reading this book, you fall into the latter group. Perhaps you're self-taught, as I was for the first few years, and you just want to make sure that you're heading in the right direction. Maybe you're a more experienced player who feels that there are some things you or your teacher simply left uncovered. But whether you're a beginner or a serious professional, I'm sure that you'll find some useful information in this book.

I've purposely tried to cover a lot of ground because this book is intended to help fill in any blanks there might be in your playing and give you a good basic understanding of the world of drumming as it is today. For this reason, there are certain areas to which an entire section – or even an entire book – could have been dedicated, but there was so much other information to cram in that it lost out. However, with the plethora of instructional aids available, there is probably an entire book dedicated to any particular subject, should you want to explore it further.

And that's the wonderful thing: I hope this book does inspire you to delve deeper into the drum kit and its possibilities. The drum kit as we know it is about only 100 years old. The hi-hat has been around for only 80-odd years, and the double pedal a mere 20 or so. It's early days. And, if you can absorb some of what's gone before, who knows where you can take it? But whether it's back to the practice room or to the stages of the world, all that matters is that you enjoy it. It is fun, after all – but you didn't need me to tell you that.

INTRODUCTION

We all have our favourite styles of music, as well as favourite grooves, licks and even tempos. But what happens when we're taken away from the comfort of these familiar friends into what, for us, is uncharted territory? I can recall a situation where it really hit home. Myself and a few friends had gone down to a jam night, and soon it was my turn to play a couple of tunes. At this point I was self-taught and, whilst not being over-confident, I felt I could play the drums, whatever that entailed. After I made a few adjustments to the kit (being a left-hander can be a drag sometimes), I turned to the keyboard player to see what we were going to play. To my surprise, he suggested a swing tune, and before I had a chance to offer any objection he was counting it off at the kind of tempo I thought was reserved for speed-metal bands. I didn't know what had hit me! I had no experience of playing jazz – or anything like it – and felt as though I could no longer play the drums. I tried keeping the spang-a-lang pattern going on the ride but lasted no longer than a few seconds before my hand cramped up. Meanwhile, the keyboard player, oblivious to (or perhaps enjoying) my humiliation, proceeded to take chorus after chorus of solos while I did my utmost to keep it together and avoid eye contact with my friends. Needless to say, I learned my lesson the hard way, but I learned it well! To call yourself a drummer really requires you to be able to play more than one style of music, not necessarily like a virtuoso, but competently. And even if you have a favourite style – whether it's funk, rock or jazz – simply understanding other styles will bring more to your drumming in terms of coordination, ideas and all-round musicality.

The material in this book covers everything from basic hand technique and co-ordination to groove-playing and soloing, all of which start with the basics and work up to the kind of level that will enable you to play in almost any musical situation. For the non-readers among you, I've tried to include on the CD audio examples of almost all of the exercises; when combined with the book, you should be able to figure out what's going on. There are, however, certain exercises I've missed out, due partly to the space restrictions of the CD but also because a particular exercise might be only a constant stream of notes with the same value (such as with Example 4 from the 'Drum Set Vocabulary' chapter, with which you can simply start slowly and work up to speed).

There's a lot of information here, so don't be put off by what you can't do. Sometimes it can be daunting to open a new book and discover how much you don't know, but remember the old Zen saying: 'A 100-mile journey starts with a single step.' Simply take it at your own pace and enjoy the view along the way. There's nothing more satisfying than learning to do something that you couldn't do the previous day, and while sometimes that progress might seem slow, with the three Ps – patience, practice and perseverance – you'll get there in the end.

Pete Riley
January 2003

1 BEFORE WE GET STARTED

'Practise every day; have a plan and stick to it. Be patient, practise new ideas slowly and quietly and develop control at many dynamic ranges and tempos.' *Steve Smith*

How many times has it happened? You go into your practice room to work through some new ideas, you start playing and before you know it you've got only five minutes' rehearsal time left. It's easy to put on a CD and play along or simply play the drums, but we're not really focusing on the areas of our playing that need the attention – it's fun to play the stuff we already know. However, if progress is going to be made, time has to be allocated to the stuff we can't do.

A few years ago, I held a drum a clinic and an old drummer friend of mine whom I hadn't seen in ten years was in the audience. At one point during the evening, I mentioned working on the areas of your playing that need attention, as opposed to simply jamming through old ideas. At the end my friend came over and said that for him I'd hit the nail on the head; while his playing hadn't really moved forward in the years since I'd seen him, he thought that I sounded like a different drummer. Obviously we need to spend some time behind the kit just playing, but it's also important to put a specific amount of time aside to work on new ideas.

'You've got be careful about what you practise. I would never want to practise something inappropriate that I would end up bringing to a gig, regurgitating it all over the stage.' *Billy Ward*

How do we know what we should be working on? I know that at certain times I've been guilty of practising things that were really not a great deal of use to my drumming while there were certain essentials that I

was neglecting. Obviously it's important that these essentials are addressed. By 'essentials', I'm referring to reading and being able to play a wide variety of styles convincingly. For example, what's the point in being able to solo in 7/8 when you can't play a great-sounding shuffle? It's exactly these sorts of essentials that are covered in this book, but after that, how do you piece it all together?

New York session player Billy Ward has a very natural way of practising. He plays a time or feel he wants to focus on, puts on a click and pretends to play a song where after, say, eight measures, he'll play a fill into a chorus, moving up to the ride and so on. As soon as he feels some friction – maybe a fill or a bass-drum pattern – he'll stop, work out what went wrong and then begin again. By practising this way, you're letting the music and your own style dictate what you work on.

'If you're not enjoying practising, go and do something else.' *Buddy Rich*

'I would say things like, "God, if I can't play for a couple of days because I'm feeling stiff, I must not be a natural drummer." But then it's learning to accept that, OK, I might feel stiff for a couple of days, but then I won't, and then I'm not pre-occupied with being faster than everyone else and practising 24 hours a day. You can do that and burn yourself out; you can just go about it the wrong way and get more frustrated, instead of doing it naturally, because of the wrong reasons.' *Vinnie Colaiuta*

Another aspect of practising that I often get asked is, 'How much practice should I do?' Well, I guess the obvious answer is, 'For as long as you're enjoying it.' I really enjoy practising; in fact, I find it one of the most rewarding aspects of drumming. But one factor to take into account is that most people can really concentrate fully for only about 20 minutes. So I tend to practise in one-hour stints which are made up of a bit of warming up and down at the beginning and end, with – hopefully – the really focused part ending up somewhere in the middle. It's often during the part at the end, where I'm just playing and enjoying it, that that new ideas appear. It seems that the release of not having to work on what's on the paper in front of you, yet having worked on some new aspects of playing, opens up the door to new possibilities. After practising for this time, I like to take a break, have a stretch and a cup of coffee and maybe listen to a recording of the stuff I've been working on (more of that later).

'I practise for three hours on most days. I find that first thing in morning, from nine to midday, is when it's most productive.' *Steve Smith*

The key here is basically to avoid overly long practice sessions, both in individual stints and over the course of a day. In the past, I've practised for 10 or even 12 hours, but I'm not sure how constructive it was. I believe that, if your practice time is constructed properly, you can achieve a good rate of progress with an hour or two a day. In fact, it's in this repetition that the answer lies. Our brains take on information better in small pieces, so spending one hour a day practising, six days a week, will yield far better results than six hours on Saturday afternoon.

'Don't practise for hours; practise for results.' *Jo Jo Meyer*

'My most productive time was during my first year of college. I had the whole summer off, I didn't know anybody, and I was up at school alone. So I made up a practice schedule, and hit it 10 to 15 hours a day for about three months.

I went through two summers of that, and it never got under six or seven hours, even when school was in session.' *Dave Weckl*

Another thing to consider is how each session is divided up. For example, suppose you have one hour in which to practise and you decide to spend five minutes on paradiddles, five minutes on jazz-time playing, five minutes on reading and so on. Firstly, you'll spend half of the session finding the right exercises and changing the tempo, but you'll also notice that progress seems slow because you're juggling so many balls at once. Instead, try dividing each hour into two or three parts and you should see results much quicker. This approach also means that you know just what it is you're going into the practice session to work on, as opposed to jamming along to a couple a CDs (a valid and important part of practising, admittedly, but it doesn't necessarily focus on the areas that need work).

Try not to neglect your responsibility to learn songs for rehearsals or gigs. It can be easy to get so involved in practising that learning new tunes gets left to the last ten minutes – and believe me, no one will comment on the fluidity of your six-stroke rolls, but they may well have something to say about your inability to remember the 2/4 measure at the end of the chorus of the new tune!

'I used to practise like a maniac, but I did back off a bit when I was around 21 because I realised that I didn't want to become some freak who couldn't play with anybody.' *Billy Ward*

The Dreaded Click

'Good time is the single most important and most difficult goal to achieve.' *Simon Phillips*

It never ceases to amaze me how many drummers never practise to a click. After all, as drummers our primary role is to state the time, although it could be argued that good time is not only our responsibility but every band member's. In this age of computer technology, people are used to hearing programmed, quantised, machine-generated accuracy, so now even the non-musician has become more unconsciously aware of metre.

'The sheer nature of the instrument is that 98 per cent of the time it's a time-keeping role. If you don't secure that role, you'll never secure a gig. The alternatives are to form your own band – then you don't have to worry about it – or go out and be a circus act. Or, better still, be a clinician!' *Dave Hassell*

This isn't to say that everything that you play needs to sound robotic; in fact, top session drummers are able to move around the click in such a way that the track has all of the push and pull of a track recorded without a click but with the beginning and end tempos remaining the same. And the fact that the drums aren't always locked in with the click isn't an issue, as the click isn't going to end up on the final recording. However, the same can't be said of sequencers, which so many bands use these days. A sequencer is essentially a machine used in the same way as a backing track, but it works using the same principle as a drum machine (ie triggering relevant sounds and samples via MIDI). But because most of what is triggered will be exactly in time – for example, tambourines or backing vocals – the drummer must remained locked in to the click or else he and the band will appear out of sync with the sequencer. There are also certain situations in which producers want a natural, live feel but at a specific tempo, so start off with a click but drop it out after the first chorus.

'I recall walking past an open studio door when a band was in session and the drummer's headphones, which were left on his stool, were practically jumping off it the click was so loud!' *Simon Phillips*

When you first try playing to a click, it can seem as if the click appears to speed up and slow down, and the common reaction is to keep turning the click up. Try to think of the click as a percussionist playing along with you, as opposed to a machine that's determined to make you look silly. To begin with, try playing simple

time along with it: eighths on the hi-hat, one and three on the bass drum and two and four on the snare. Once this is feeling good, try adding a simple fill every few measures. You'll eventually reach the point where you stop noticing the click, allowing it to go lower and lower in the mix. When I was touring with pop band Republica, all of the live show was played to a sequencer, so I had a click on every tune. The previous drummer had just the click in his monitor, which to me makes for a very odd mix; instead I had a bit of all of the sequenced parts, the rest of the band and the click mixed together, sometimes to the point at which it was hard to discern the click from the music, but it all blended to create a really musical mix.

Recording Yourself

'Always record yourself. Don't play anywhere without making a tape. I think it's imperative that you record your gigs. You need that recording to be able to go back and hear what you made the audience and bandmates sit through! I'm sorry, the tape doesn't lie.' *Billy Ward*

I remember the first time I recorded some of the exercises I was practising at the time. I couldn't believe what I was hearing: it sounded lumpy, inaccurate and just plain ungroovy, yet when I was playing them it felt fine. It's funny how our perception of what we're playing can be different from what it actually sounds like. Every gigging musician has some nights when they feel their playing was great but no one comments on it, and others where they feel it was particularly poor but get compliments on it nonetheless! Obviously, some of this is subjective, but the point is that, unless you're able to hear it and make your own judgment, how will you know? A cheap tape recorder is a really useful practice tool in this respect; after all, how do you think session players such as Steve Gadd got so good? It's simply through hearing themselves on tape all the time. Well, that and a bit of practice!

Mini Studio

My recording facilities have moved on somewhat since my initial investment in a tape recorder, but the point is that you don't need to spend a fortune to have a really practical recording set-up. Another really useful investment is a pair of isolation headphones. When I first used a pair, I couldn't believe how I'd managed for so long without them. Basically, isolation headphones consist of a set of ear defenders with speaker drivers fitted. This means that the acoustic drum sound is reduced by the specified amount, usually upwards of 20dB, which in turn means that the music or click can be monitored at a much lower volume. This enables you to hear clearly all of the detail in the music – and it also saves your ears. If you plug the iso-phones into the tape recorder as you record, you can also hear the miked version of your kit, which adds clarity to the slightly muffled sound caused by the iso-phones. This gives you the best of both worlds: a quieter drum sound but with clarity.

The next step you could consider is the purchase of a mixing desk, and it doesn't have be the dining-room-table-sized affair found in most large studios. These days several companies, such as Mackie and Behringer, make small notepad desks that are about the sizes of laptop computers. These are compact, simplified versions of their bigger brothers, with a lot of the same features. Things to look out for are XLR inputs and phantom powering (see Chapter 8, 'In The Studio'). A desk with four XLRs would be an ideal starting point although more is OK. This will enable you to plug in up to four mics. You can now EQ and blend the mics, which you can monitor in the iso-phones. You can also plug drum machines, drum modules and CD, tape or MiniDisk players into the desk. Any of the last three can also be plugged in to record from the desk. This is the fun part. Now you're able to hear yourself playing along with CDs or clicks, or maybe even other band members, if you have enough inputs.

These desks also have auxiliary inputs that enable you to add effects, such as reverb, to the drums. So, for the price of a new snare drum, you're able to create your own studio environment in your own practice room. This is a fantastic practice tool and a great way of honing your drumming and studio skills.

Togetherness, Placement, Dynamics

Aside from their ability to find the right part for a song as well as record it within a couple of takes, part of what makes top session players so in demand is their ability to make everything flow. Try to listen for these same attributes in your own playing when you're practising. For example, when you play two or more sounds together, are they really falling *exactly* together? This can be much more difficult than it sounds, especially when you get into the realms of four-way coordination.

The placement of notes is also crucial. For example, if you're playing a broken or linear-style groove, because you no longer have the reference of the right hand playing an ostinato, such as eighth notes, it's much easier to play notes slightly early or late. Dynamics can also play a part in this. For example, when I was working on getting dynamics into my playing, I recorded a take which I then listened back to. I'd accented the quarter notes on the hi-hats and played the upbeat eighth notes much quieter, but the tune, which was a straight eighth-note rock tune, felt uncomfortable. It felt like the upbeat eighth notes were late in relation to the quarter notes, even though they were in the right place. This is because quieter notes can sound later and louder notes earlier. In this case, the track would have been much better served with more evenly accented eighths driving it along. Again, as with all of this stuff, recording yourself will help.

Ear Today...

Drums are, by nature, one of the loudest acoustic instruments, capable of giving out decibel levels the kind of which most health-and-safety officials would deem unsafe. Cymbals and snare drums are especially dangerous, with the high frequencies inherent to their sounds capable of dealing out permanent hearing damage. A friend of mine – a successful player and teacher – actually had to give up playing altogether after developing tinnitus and hyperacusis.

Tinnitus is the ringing sensation we feel after being subjected to loud noise. This usually goes away within a few hours but in some cases it stays – for good. The ringing can also come in the form of whistling, bells chiming or, in the case of my right ear when a room is particularly quiet, Morse code.

Hyperacusis is even worse. Basically, your ears

become hypersensitive, making even the most inoffensive noises, such as a car engine or a TV, feel painfully loud. Although symptoms may recede, it's usually the case that, once the damage is done, it's irreversible. If it sounds like I'm painting a particularly bleak picture here, it's because I intend to. Hearing-damage is no fun, and the silly thing is that it's easy to prevent. There are various hearing-protection products on the market, from cheap foam earplugs to custom-moulded ones, as well as isolation headphones, ear defenders and in-ear monitors. I have a pair of custom-moulded plugs that reduce the sound heard by 15dB. This tends to take the edge off things, making situations that are a bit too loud more tolerable. I recall Radiohead drummer Phil Selway telling me that he wears them whenever he plays, saying that they clean up the sound when it's loud and muddy both in the studio and on stage.

That's not to say that you need to play with your earplugs in all the time. If you're playing at a realistic volume, in a reasonably sized room, you should be able to play without plugs by playing the drums at the appropriate volume for the room. At a recent masterclass in a particularly live, reverberant room, Steve Smith stressed the importance of playing for the room, as opposed to simply getting up there and playing at your usual volume. But in situations where it's just too loud, I recommend using some kind of earplug or, if it's in your own practice space, you could try ear defenders, available from most DIY stores. These are more comfortable than most earplugs and tend to give the kit a nice, compressed sound. And even better than the ear defenders are the isolation headphones mentioned earlier. Whichever you choose, it will be a worthwhile investment – after all, we only get one set of ears, and once they're damaged, there's no second chance.

Warming Up

When asked if he did any limbering up for a show, Buddy Rich's response was, 'Yeah, I usually take my hands out of my pockets.' For the rest of us, some amount of warming up is usually essential, if not to get the hands working together then to get the blood flowing and help prevent injury. I often hear drummers ask how they should warm up, and to me the first thing – sometimes the only thing – I find necessary is literally warming my hands. I'm cursed with poor circulation, and if my hands are cold I can't feel the sticks. A few minutes near a heater usually works, but I've heard of other musicians immersing their hands in hot water before going on stage – whatever it takes, I suppose. If I have a pad to hand, I'll work through a few rudiments, starting out slowly, just feeling the sticks rebounding, then picking up the speed.

I also like to warm up before practising. I'll start with an ostinato with the feet and begin adding some simple figures with the hands: singles, doubles, paradiddles and so on. I find the ostinato helps get the blood flowing, the co-ordination gets the brain working and whatever figures the hands are playing helps to warm them up. The key to all of this is to remember what this process is for and not to dive straight in. Start slow and stay relaxed.

No Pain, No Strain

'Drumming is definitely not a track-and-field event.' *Billy Ward*

If at any point during warming up or playing you feel any pain, stop. This is your body's way of telling you that you're either doing damage or it's already done. Drums are a very physical instrument, with some of today's rock players looking more like they're trying to knock the drum kit through the drum riser rather than playing the instrument, so it's easy to see why injuries can occur. Some common sense here is all you need. Some people are built to take the abuse that this kind of playing requires, but some of us aren't. Play at the dynamic you feel comfortable with, and if that means your backbeat stroke starts from somewhere behind your head, that's fine, but consider the fact that, while it might look cool, it probably doesn't sound any better.

Volume isn't the only cause of injuries; the quest for speed can also cause problems. If you do succumb to one of the classic drummer ailments, such as tendonitis, RSI (Repetitive Strain Injury) or carpel tunnel syndrome, the best remedy is to put down the sticks, take a break and let the body get on with repairing itself. If there's no respite, there are specialists who deal with these ailments, but ideally prevention is better than cure and one of the best ways to avoid injury is to develop your technique and get the sticks working for you.

2 SET-UP AND TECHNIQUE

'I once saw the cellist Rostropovich at the University of Indiana. He just strode across the stage during the applause, sat right down and as soon as his bottom touched the seat, he was playing. And the cello was part of him – he was the cello.' *Peter Erskine*

How we sit in relation to the kit can greatly affect how our ideas are allowed to flow. If you're leaning to either side, it can be difficult to remain balanced, yet it's surprising how many drummers lean towards the hi-hat or over the snare. This not only affects your balance but it's also a great way of developing a serious back problem some way down the line! Also, try to keep your shoulders and, of course, your whole body relaxed. Thinking about your breathing can help here, and whenever I feel under pressure when playing, a few deep breaths and relaxing the shoulders always helps to relieve any tension.

At this stage, let's try to set up the kit from scratch, starting with the drum throne. The best method I've encountered for maintaining good posture involves sitting towards the front of the throne, where, because the backs of the thighs are no longer supported, you're no longer able to slouch. This in turn forces the top of the back outwards, creating a straighter back.

Another factor in developing good posture is stool height. If it's too high, you can feel unstable and distant from the kit; too low and lifting the legs can soon become hard work. There are, of course, some drummers who play in this way. For example, Vinnie Colaiuta admits to sitting really low in his early days, and he didn't sound too bad! Another example could be Tony Williams, who sat really high in comparison. Of course, there are no hard and fast rules, and the only answer is to experiment, but aim to keep the thighs at right angles to the floor when the feet are on the pedals (in the heel-up position, if you play heel-up).

Now you're sitting comfortably, it's time to consider the pedals and your distance from them. This might not be something you've given a lot of thought to until now, but a lot of drummers sit very close to the kit, which might seem logical but can play havoc with pedal technique. For example, try sitting close to the kit so that your knees are at less than right angles. Now try playing some simple patterns in a heel-down position. I'm sure you'll soon find your shins burning! Now try positioning your bass drum and hi-hat at a more comfortable distance, maybe sitting towards the edge of the throne at the same time.

Now would be a good time to consider pedal placement, but before we do, let's consider this idea of being centred again, this time by establishing where the centre of the kit is. If you take a single-bass-drum kit, a lot of drummers – and non drummers – could be forgiven for considering the bass drum as the centre, but it's not. The snare drum should be regarded as the centre, with the pedals placed at comfortable positions on either side. This idea of the bass drum being central is probably the reason for a lot of the leaning mentioned earlier – because the bass drum is facing the front, the drummer tries to face that way.

'Sit down as though you're sitting down to eat. Your feet should fall at a natural distance apart from one another. That's why I place my hi-hat pedal inside my double pedal – I want to keep my legs in the position they feel most comfortable.' *Billy Ward*

Now that we're heading in the right direction, let's add the snare drum. A couple of points to consider here are the height and angle. A lot of younger drummers tend to position their snares low and steeply angled towards them. If the drum's too low, your hands tend to hit your legs before the drum, but if the drum is too high, it can cause you to hit the rim of the drum harder than you'd necessarily prefer. This can cause pain at worst but can also thin out the sound of the drum. A good general rule of thumb would be to have the drum somewhere between the tops of your legs and waist height.

Also, consider the angle at which the stick meets the drum. If the drum is angled towards the drummer but at an angle, it can make it difficult – if not impossible – to play rimshots (simultaneously hitting the centre and the rim of the drum) comfortably. It's also very difficult for the stick to rebound off the drum when the stick-to-head attitude is this extreme. You can try this by loosely dropping the tip of a stick on a worktop from a relatively flat angle. Now try the same thing with the hand six inches above the worktop and you'll feel the stick simply die, with virtually no rebound at all. The drum should be placed at an angle that enables the stick to rebound easily and rimshots to be played.

This idea of reducing the angle between the stick and the playing surface applies to the whole of the kit. It can feel really apparent on the ride cymbal, where, as the angle increases, the response of the cymbal decreases, as gravity simply wants to pull the stick through the hand, as opposed to acting upon the tip.

Set-Up

'I can look at a kit and half tell what a drummer's going to sound like.' *Peter Erskine*

Experiment with angles and heights as you add the toms and cymbals, and remember, as Billy Ward says, 'Don't set your kit up as they do in the catalogues!'. We're all different, so what works for one person may feel uncomfortable to another. Don't be afraid of placing the drums and cymbals where they feel comfortable, but do be aware of being able to maintain eye contact with the rest of the band. I recall some friends of mine playing with Nicko McBrain from rock band Iron Maiden, who used nine toms and about twice as many cymbals, and when he was on the riser they simply couldn't see him to get cues. Well, at least it was a good excuse for any mistakes they might have made!

'You can take one snare and one tom and right there you've got infinite possibilities.' *Elvin Jones*

While enormous kits might look impressive, they can be a distraction; it's easy to feel obliged to use every available sound simply because it's there. Often, far more impressive is the drummer who can say more with less. For the majority of his career, Steve Gadd used three cymbals and a hi-hat. Or how about the jazz drummers of the '50s and '60s? Here, a four-piece kit with two cymbals was the norm and drummers such as Tony Williams, Elvin Jones and Roy Haynes really said more on those set-ups than most of us can with twice as many drums and cymbals!

'I decided to take just two cymbals and a hi-hat on a month-long tour after watching a video of the Miles Davis band with Tony Williams playing with only two cymbals. Less was definitely more.' *Peter Erskine*

If you're used to playing a larger set-up, try stripping down to a four-piece every so often – it can be a refreshing change and a new challenge. That isn't to say that all drummers who use large set-ups are hiding their inadequacies behind a wall of gear, of course. Players such as Simon Phillips and Terry Bozzio have not only developed the restraint and taste to use these set-ups musically but they also play in situations that enable them to utilise all of those sounds.

Technique

'It's about freeing up the hands so you can have a certain kind of touch and elicit that kind of touch out of the instrument so you don't have to think whether or not you can do it any more, and then you can become one with the instrument.' *Vinnie Colaiuta*

A lot of people tend to confuse vocabulary with technique, saying things such as, 'Oh, he's always showing off his technique. He never shuts up.' When we play, we're *always* showing our technique. Technique is the way in which we play the instrument, the motions we use and how they flow. Our vocabulary is what we have to say. A great exponent of both of these areas is Steve Smith. His playing looks amazing – it flows beautifully, with the sticks apparently defying gravity, while his vocabulary is seemingly endless! Steve's vocabulary would take a whole series of books, so let's instead begin by establishing what makes good technique.

'Technique has been my tool to help me make my statement, but my statement comes from my spirit.' *Vinnie Colaiuta*

Grip

'If a student comes to me for a lesson, I don't make any changes to their grip unless it's really hindering them.' *Billy Ward*

First, let's establish the three basic grips and their differences. Probably the most commonly used grip these days is the *matched grip*. (This could be credited to Ringo's appearance on *The Ed Sullivan Show* all those years ago, because up until then most drummers played traditional grip, or orthodox grip as it's also called.) Matched grip is exactly as it sounds, with both hands holding the stick the same way, with the stick passing through the hand and supported between the fingers and the pad of the thumb.

There are two variations of the matched grip: French and German. French – or *French timpani*, to give it its proper name – involves the thumbnails pointing straight up, allowing the fingers good access to the stick. German, on the other hand, has the thumbs pointing at each other. Personally, I find somewhere in between the two most comfortable, as the twist in the German grip feels unnatural and an unnecessary effort while the position of the French grip – although it makes finger-control easy – makes accenting difficult because the wrist simply doesn't work that way.

'Traditional grip is the hardest thing you'll ever learn.' *Bob Armstrong*

Traditional grip is what the drum kit was originally developed around and originated from military marching drummers who, with drums slung across their fronts or to the side, would find matched grip impossible. It seems that, when the various elements of the drum kit as we know it came together, no one questioned the basic grip and it remained the grip of choice until the advent of rock 'n' roll. As volumes crept up, however, the switch to matched grip was a natural one.

So why, then, do so many great drummers insist on sticking with such a seemingly archaic way of playing the kit? There are a couple of reasons. Firstly, traditional grip enables you to play delicately much more easily than matched grip because the hand is below the stick. You need only to lay the stick across the edge of your hand, where the thumb joins, and allow it to bounce on the drum. You can feel immediately how loose and light the grip can be. Secondly, because the grips in both hands are so different, it creates a sort of lead/follow feeling that really lends itself to certain situations – jazz, for example.

To hold the stick in traditional grip, try holding out your hand as though you're about to hold a bag of sugar and lay the stick across the hand from the base of the thumb to the tip of the third finger. If you now roll your hand inwards through 90 degrees, you have the basic playing position. For lighter playing, the arm simply rotates at the elbow, while for louder strokes the arm creates a whipping motion akin to that of flicking water from the tips of your fingers. With a little pressure, the stick is kept in place between the thumb and the hand, where it pivots and is supported by the third finger, on which it sits at the third joint. The little finger isn't used at all in this technique and the second finger simply sits lightly on the stick most of the time. In basic terms, the power comes from the thumb while control comes from the index finger (although drummers such as Elvin Jones and Jack De Johnette mostly use their thumbs, and players such as Vinnie Colaiuta and Steve Smith also incorporate their forefingers).

Strike The Balance

When I was younger I'd sit through various drum videos until it reached the part where the drummer inevitably began to talk about how he holds the sticks. At this point I'd reach for the remote and forward past it. As a young drummer, how I held the sticks seemed irrelevant – I could hit the drums, I was happy. As time went on, however, I discovered that there was more to this drumming lark than simply hitting things. I needed some control. If I was going to play double, single and buzz strokes I needed to get the stick working for me, and the first thing I needed to establish was the balance point of the stick.

Holding the stick at the balance point can really help the stick to feel alive and responsive. To do this, try another worktop experiment: support the stick with only the forefinger and hold it right at the end. Now try dropping the tip onto the worktop. You should feel the stick die with very little bounce. This is because you're behind the balance point. Now try holding the stick nearer the middle, dropping the stick again. This time the stick will be reluctant to bounce, as you're too far in front of the balance point. Finally, hold the stick with about an inch or so of the butt of the stick showing out of the heel of the hand and try dropping the stick again. It should bounce easily, as you're probably fairly close to the balance point. But what happens if you grip the stick? Chances are it's a little less likely to bounce.

OK, but now try throwing the stick down from about six inches or so. Does it return to its starting height? If not, you're probably gripping the stick too tightly.

'The stick should be placed in the hand as though you're holding a bird: too loose and it would fly away, too tight and it would choke the bird.' *Dave Hassell*

Try getting the stick to rebound back to its starting point. This can seem really alien at first, especially if you're used to playing into the drums, but it can really help to create fluid, tension-free drumming. Try the 'stop at the top' exercise below. In matched grip, try to keep the hands and fingers in their usual positions. In traditional grip, try leaving it all to the thumb – this will work for most medium tempos. At quicker speeds, the fingers can be used to help things along.

Example 1

Fingers

After a few years of drumming, I was lucky enough to attend a masterclass with renowned educator Gary Chaffee. Towards the end of the class, Gary got each of the students to play a groove in various styles, and whilst a few of us struggled to determine the difference between a salsa and a samba, it was being told to get all of my fingers on the sticks that had the most immediate effect. I'd developed the bad habit of keeping my 'pinkies' off the stick and had underestimated – or simply not considered – how important a role all of the fingers play. If you need more convincing, consider the fact that there are mountain climbers who are able to support their own weight using individual fingers! That's not to say that the fingers shouldn't come off the sticks at some point – when playing buzz or press rolls, for example – and when playing lightly on the ride I'll often end up using just the first two fingers, giving the stick the freedom to move.

To help develop strength and control in the fingers, try holding the stick in the French timpani position (with the thumb on top) and, using only the fingers – no wrist – try to get the stick bouncing on the drum. Eventually you should be able to move all of the fingers at the right speed to perpetuate the bounce of the stick.

This can also work with traditional grip and from two different positions. First, while holding the stick in the regular traditional position, roll the hand over so that the palm is facing the floor. Now the first two fingers should be over the stick and these can be used to keep the stick moving. Alternatively, from the regular position again, this time roll the hand back through 90 degrees so that the palm is facing upwards. Again, the first two fingers can now be used to bounce the stick. Once you can get each hand working like this, try bringing the hands together, playing a single-stroke roll in the same way.

These finger-control exercises can take some work to refine, but you should really start to feel a difference in your overall hand technique as a result.

The Moeller System

Sanford Augustus Moeller was born in the 1880s and, while observing different drummers (including soldiers from the Civil War), he noticed a relationship between speed and power and the motions they used. He actually wrote a book on the subject but felt that the accompanying pictures didn't carry the message clearly enough. Fortunately, however, he did teach his approach to some influential players, including Jim Chapin, whose playing is still a fine example of the technique today.

During the last few years, there's been much talk about the Moeller 'system', and although it seems to have been interpreted in various ways by different drummers and teachers, the basic principles are the same. It's basically a way of breaking down the mechanics of playing accented and unaccented notes into individual strokes. By doing this, it's possible always to have the sticks in the right place for the next stroke. And by harnessing the rebound of the stick for accented strokes and also playing quieter 'tap' strokes, as the sticks move upwards to prepare for the next accent, a 'graceful economy of movement' is created.

In its simplest form, the 'system' can be broken down into four strokes: tap strokes (T), full strokes (F), upstrokes (U) and downstrokes (D). In the 'stop at the top' exercise, we were actually working on the full stroke (sometimes called the free stroke), which is probably the most difficult to develop. It could be likened to playing an accent in a single movement, which at certain speeds most of us actually do. For example, if you play hand-to-hand single-stroke 16th notes at, say, 116bpm (beats per minute), as long as you allow the sticks to rebound you're probably using some kind of full stroke. If, however, you play eighth notes at the same tempo, there's a fair chance – assuming you've never worked on the stroke – that you'll be playing each stroke as two separate movements: the first bringing the stick down to hit the drum, the second lifting the stick back up to the starting point. So now try the same thing but feeling the rebound and life in the stick and playing each hit in one movement.

The (tap stroke could actually be regarded as a smaller version of the full stroke. This is going to be our 'ghosted' or unaccented note. It should be played from a height of around one half to one inch off the drum; as with the full stroke the stick should start and end its movement at the top. You could try playing some slow singles, doubles and paradiddles to work on this once each hand is starting to feel good. One thing to be aware of, though, is to avoid lifting the hand to prepare for the stroke. You can practise this by placing your other stick over the top so that you'll hit the sticks together if you lift the stick first.

The downstroke is straightforward enough. This is our accented note, but it stops at the bottom, ready to play an unaccented note. The one important element to develop here is the ability to stop the stick about one-half to one inch off the drum once the stroke has been played. To do this, simply snap the stick into the hand the instant the stick impacts with the head. Then the hand immediately relaxes again. Just try throwing the stick down from your normal accent height – say, about 8–12 inches off the drum – and killing the stroke dead at the bottom. As you can see, this is completely the reverse of the full stroke, the difference being that the full stroke plays an accent and prepares for and allows you to play another accented note after it, whereas after the accent in the downstroke the stick stays low to play an unaccented note.

The final stroke is the upstroke. This motion really characterises the Moeller system with its flowing movement as it lifts the stick from low to high to play an accent. One of the best analogies for developing this movement is if you sit at the kit with your arms relaxed in front you, then slowly shake your hands as if to shake water off the tips of your fingers. If you're relaxed, you should feel the movement starting from the elbow, moving down through the wrist to the ends of the fingers. This motion actually comprises two of our strokes: the up, as it lifts the stick, and the down, as it returns to the low starting point.

Now try the same thing with a stick. You should hopefully be feeling a sort of whipping motion. Like all of these strokes, this can take some time to develop, but another way of working on it can be to play eighth notes on the hi-hat with accents on the quarter notes. The quarter notes are our downstrokes and the eighths our up strokes.

As you do this, try playing the accented notes on the edges of the cymbals using the shoulder of the stick and the unaccented notes on the top using the tip of the stick. This can really help to develop the movement in a natural way. In fact, a lot of drummers do this hi-hat motion instinctively.

Once you've familiarised yourself with the individual strokes, it's time to start piecing them together. Below are some basic accenting exercises that are to be played with each hand individually. Try working on these at 60bpm. This may seem slow, but it really gives you time absorb the motions.

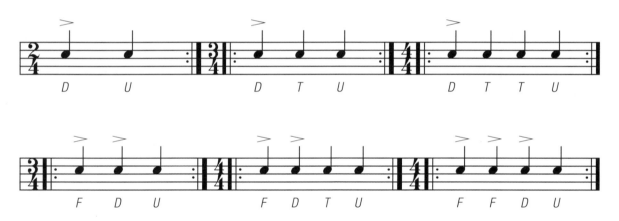

Example 2

The first three sections of Example 2 can also be played much faster to create a classic Moeller exercise. Each of these examples can be played very quickly, allowing the energy within the stick after the accent is played to play the remaining notes. This should feel as though only the accent is being played. A challenging exercise you can try with this is to play one of the figures in the left hand on the snare and solo over it with the right.

Now it's time to bring the two hands together. Example 3a uses single strokes with one accent which moves one eighth note to the right in each subsequent exercise. These first four examples should also be practised leading with the left hand. The exercises in 3b again use single strokes but now, as we're dealing with eighth-note triplets, the accents move hand to hand. The third exercise looks deceptively easy, but it really is quite difficult to master, especially at slower tempos. In the third set of exercises, 3c, all use the same basic paradiddle sticking – RLRR, LRLL – only now, like in the first example, the accent moves one note to the right each time. As simple as this sounds it plays havoc with the motions required, so be sure to stay slow and focus on the movements.

Try to apply these same principles to all of the exercises in the book and I'm sure you'll soon begin to feel a new looseness and fluidity in your playing.

Also, be sure to check out some of the great exponents of these techniques, as it makes so much more sense when you're able to see this stuff in action. Players such as Steve Smith, Dom Famularo, Buddy Rich, Joe Morello and Vinnie Colaiuta are a good starting point.

Example 3a

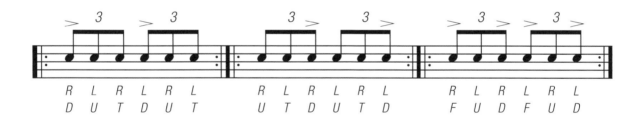

Example 3b

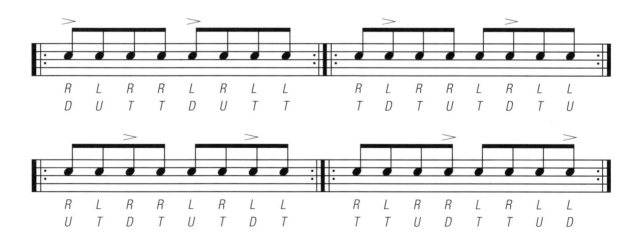

Example 3c

Bass-Drum Technique

There are two commonly used approaches to playing the bass drum, heel-up or heel-down, and personally I think it can be useful to be able to play a bit of both. For example, in most rock/pop/funk situations, heel-up feels natural and gives the necessary volume, whereas in a quiet situation – perhaps when playing some straightahead jazz – it can feel uncomfortable to support the whole leg in a heel-up position, so heel-down feels best. The other important thing to consider is what happens to the beater once the bass drum is hit.

'I've found that the best way to get a great sound on the drum is to pull the bass-drum beater off the head immediately, not forcing it up against the head.' *Simon Phillips*

Burying the beater into the head can choke the sound of the drum, especially on more open-tuned bass drums, so allowing the beater to rebound off the head gives a bigger sound. Also, if the heel is dropped back onto the heelplate immediately after the beater hits it enables the leg to relax. Allowing the beater to rebound will work with both heel-up and heel-down techniques. Try developing this approach by playing a simple groove with the snare on 2 and 4 and the kick on 1 and 3 and focus on exactly how the bass drum is being played. As you get more comfortable, add a few more notes to the bass drum. Once it begins to feel natural, try working through the bass-drum/hi-hat examples in Chapter 5, 'Drum Set Vocabulary'.

Hi-Hat Technique

The hi-hat can also be played with the heel up or down. If the time is being played on the hi-hat and an open sound is needed, to me it feels odd to lift the whole of the leg unless a short, open sound such as a 16th note is needed. If, however, I'm pedalling time with the left foot while playing the ride, heel-up enables the leg to bounce on the ball of the foot, helping to perpetuate the feel. If playing 2 and 4 with the left foot in, say, a jazz context, the rocking motion discussed in the 'Swing' section of the 'Time Playing' chapter feels best as it gives the leg something to do in between beats 2 and 4, creating a nice motion. It also locks in with the bass drum, if it's playing quarter notes.

To splash the hi-hat, you can either keep the heel on the heelplate, splashing the cymbals by pushing the toes down, or keep the toes lightly in place on the footboard and drop the heel onto the heelplate. Another technique that can be used is opening and closing the cymbals by alternating between the splashed sound (by dropping the heel) and the closed sound, with the heel up. This can sound effective when playing the ride cymbal, sounding almost as though you've grown another hand that's playing the hi-hat.

When incorporating these ideas into your playing, try saving them for the practice room until they really feel a part of you. When playing with other musicians, you want to be playing music and not thinking about technique or whether you're holding your sticks correctly. Obviously, there are some points you might want to address, but these are things that you can correct in an instant – as opposed to spending an entire gig or rehearsal looking at your bass-drum foot!

3 RUDIMENTS

'It seems to me that these days a lot of drummers are focusing on developing control with the feet but snare-drum technique is being neglected.' *Steve Smith*

If you were to ask players of Steve's generation about their early years, you'd probably find that most of them started out playing snare drum first. In fact, there are several stories of teachers not even allowing young drummers to have kits until they'd completed a year or two of just playing the snare drum. This approach seems harsh by modern standards – now most drummers get a kit, put on the latest CD and they're off! I think this idea of playing music from the beginning is valid, as you're immediately learning skills, such as what the drummer's role is within the music, but after that there is only so much that can be done without developing a certain degree of coordination between the hands.

These days, while a lot of emphasis is put on developing four-way coordination, perhaps developing some two-way coordination between the hands could be a better place to start. I think that part of the problem here is that some drummers are deterred from working on rudiments, as it can be hard to find a situation in which you can apply this sort of snare-drum material – after all, breaking into some Philly Jo Jones licks in the middle of a rock tune would sound more than a little out of context, but the control, accuracy and endurance that you'd gain from working through this sort of material is invaluable. You could compare it to jogging: no one needs to run in this day and age, yet it can feel good to do it (sometimes!) and it makes you feel more alert and stronger. The same could be said of rudiments. I don't think I've ever played a flamacue in a song, but working through a few played hand to hand is a great exercise that requires good coordination and technique.

In this chapter you'll find some of my old favourites from the 26 rudiments, but I've also chucked in some more modern ways of working through things such as singles, flams and double strokes. I've purposely focused on only those rudiments and concepts that apply well to the kit without sounding too much like snare-drum exercises.

Before we start, just a word about working through these – and similar – exercises: personally, I like to begin playing this stuff on a practice pad. It gets rid of the distraction of the rest of the kit, and it's also easier on the ears! Also, although the idea is to eventually whip these exercises up to speed, begin slowly – really slowly – and be sure that your sticking and dynamics are accurate.

Rolls

Let's begin with some basics. First up, the single-stroke roll. This can be practised in several ways. First, we can begin slowly, working it up to speed (Example 1). When doing this, try starting with full strokes, feeling the rebound in the sticks. As the tempo builds, start involving the fingers until eventually you should be able to feel just the fingers doing almost all of the work. The chances are you'll feel things getting a little tricky as the tempo builds, with the culprit probably being your weaker hand. One exercise that you can try here is to play 16th notes with the right hand counting bars up to 25, so you'll have played 100. Obviously, it's a good idea to start at a tempo at which you stand a chance of ending the exercise, perhaps 80bpm. Then try the same thing with the opposite hand. Once you can reach 100 with either hand, try playing single-stroke 32nd notes, now counting with the right hand up to 100 again.

Example 1

Example 2

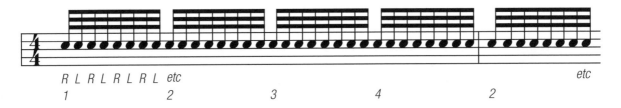

Example 3

Now let's try double strokes, or the long roll (Example 4). This is probably one of the most commonly misplayed strokes, with a lot of drummers simply allowing the stick to bounce to create the second stroke. Unfortunately, the laws of physics dictate that the second stroke is going to be quieter than the first, which creates a lumpy, uneven sound. Instead, we need to develop the ability to play the second stroke as loudly as the first.

Take a look at the next exercises. In Example 5, the right hand is playing a shuffle-type figure with the emphasis on the beat. Next, the left hand is added on the second partial of the triplet. The next step is to double the left hand to create four evenly spaced 16th notes, and finally the second note in the right hand is accented to create inverted, or displaced, double strokes. Once this can be played accurately, try moving the sticking from RLLR to the regular sticking, RRLL. This sounds a little odd as you start off but once the tempo builds, you'll hear the dynamics smoothe out. From a technical standpoint, try snapping the stick into the hand using the fingers on the second stroke.

Try moving between single and double stroke in both 16th and eighth-note-triplet subdivisions (Example 6).

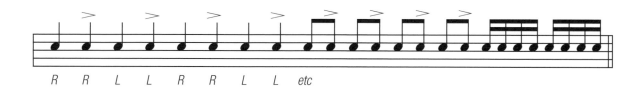

Example 4

Example 5

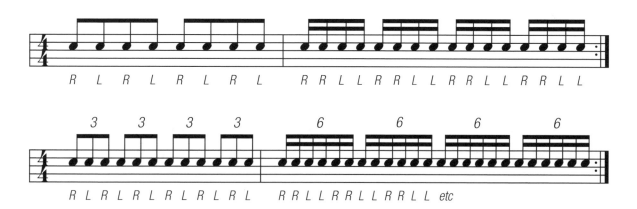

Example 6

Accenting

'My teacher, Max Abrams, used to say that he didn't want to be able to hear the unaccented notes.' *Neal Wilkinson*

In this section, we're going to take a look at a way of interpreting figures as accents within single, double and flam strokes. By looking at these different concepts in this way, it actually enables you to phrase within them, as opposed to being locked into a particular figure. For example, if you look at all of the different double-stroke rolls within the 26 rudiments – 7, 9, 11 and so on – it can be difficult to apply them in a natural way, whereas if you can simply place accents at any point within a double stroke it offers much more flexibility.

Firstly, let's take a look at some basic single-stroke examples. All of the even groups should be played leading with either hand, but obviously the odd groups switch hands so both hands gets worked on. Start each exercise really slowly, being sure to achieve a big difference in dynamics between the accented and unaccented notes in Example 7. Once these are flowing, try the permutation exercises shown in Example 8. In the first example, single accents permutate one 16th note to the right in each measure. In the next, two accents.

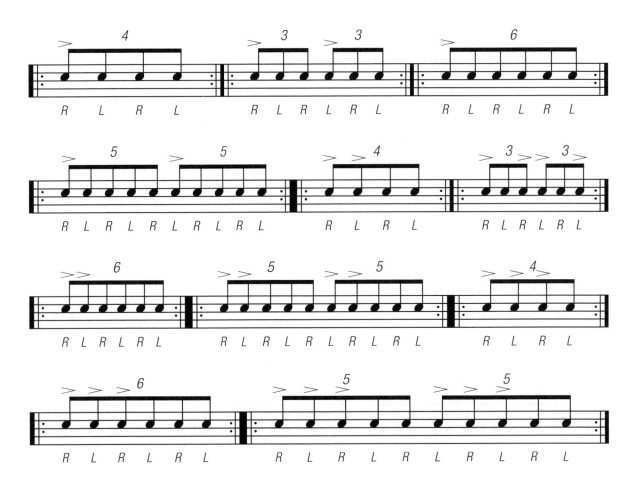

Example 7

Now let's try the same exercises again, but this time replacing the unaccented notes with double strokes. These should be played quietly, at the same volume as the original single strokes. The other important thing to note is that we're not doubling the accented notes; they remain in the original 16th-note subdivision.

Notice how our first two original figures, which had one accent in a group of three and four respectively, have now become seven- and five-stroke rolls. Again, all of the even groups should be played leading with

Example 8

the opposite hand (Example 9). Once these are feeling comfortable, try applying the same principle to the permutation exercises.

Once you're able to play these exercises comfortably, the next step is to learn how to phrase with them. Let's take the following four bars of reading text in Example 10, which we're going to play as accents within single strokes in Example 11. Now let's double the unaccented notes. Notice again how the accents remain in the original 16th-note subdivision, with only the unaccented notes being played as 32nd notes, as shown in Example 12.

We can begin to apply these examples to the kit with some simple orchestration ideas. Firstly, you could try placing all right-hand accents on the floor tom and all left-hand accents on the hi tom. Secondly, try playing the bass drum and right- and left-hand cymbals on all accents.

The same kind of approach can be applied to triplets. Again, let's take some reading text. Here we have some eighth- and quarter-note-based text, which we're going to interpret with a swing feel (Example 13). (For more details on swing interpretation, have a look at Example 5 in the 'Swing Playing' section, Chapter 4.) For now, all that we need to remember is that any note falling on an upbeat eighth note will fall on the third partial of the triplet.

Let's begin by interpreting it as accents within single-stroke eighth-note-triplets (Example 14). The most difficult thing to come to terms with is the way the quarter-note accents move hand to hand. Next up, let's double the unaccented notes (Example 15).

To help you begin to apply these ideas, be sure to try the orchestration ideas suggested earlier. Another thing that can help tie things together is splashing the hi-hat with the left foot on quarter notes.

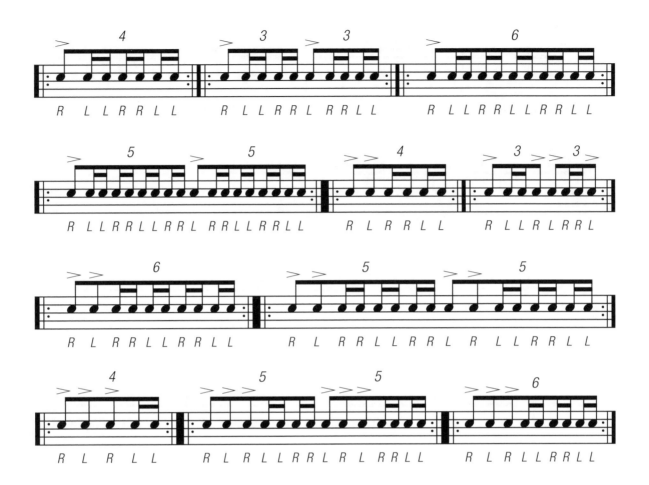

Example 9

Example 10

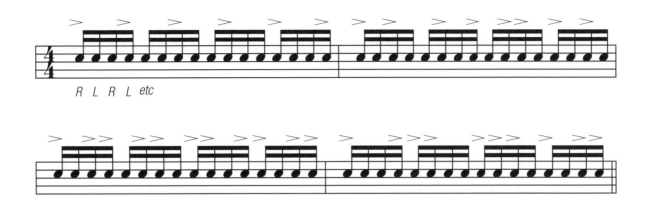

Example 11

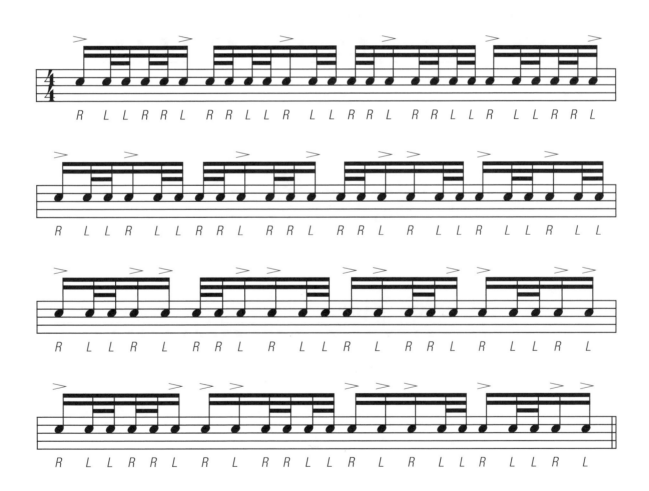

Example 12

Example 13

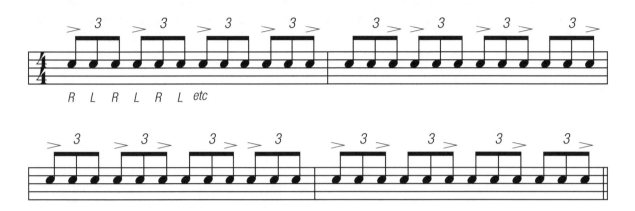

R L R L R L *etc*

Example 14

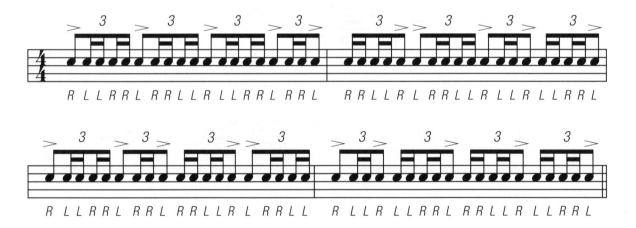

R L L R R L R R L L R L L R R L R R L   R R L L R L R R L L R L L R L L R R L

R L L R R L R R L R R L L R L R R L L   R L L R L L R R L R R L L R L L R R L

Example 15

Paradiddles

It's easy to underestimate the importance of paradiddles within today's kit-playing, especially when they're just approached from a 'RLRRLRLL-play-it-as-quick-as-you-can' angle. Where on Earth are you going to use that? Let's take a look at some basic paradiddle stickings and apply some dynamics to them. Here are the basic single, double and triple paradiddles as well as the paradiddle-diddle and paradiddle-diddle-diddle-diddle variants (Examples 16–20).

Example 16

Example 17

Example 18

Example 19

Example 20

You could then try applying them in different subdivisions to those in which you'd expect to play them. For example, the basic paradiddle is a four-note grouping so it feels very natural played within 16th notes, where the accents will fall on quarter notes (Example 21).

Example 21

But what happens if we play them within a triplet subdivision? The accents should begin to accent the half-note triplet, giving a three-over-four polyrhythm. Example 22 takes two bars to resolve.

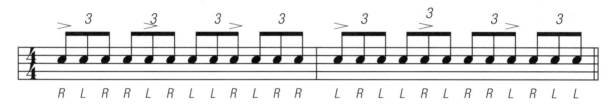

Example 22

We could do the same thing with the paradiddle-diddle-diddle, which takes two bars to resolve back to beat 1 but four bars to resolve back to the right hand. Example 23 accents the whole-note triplet.

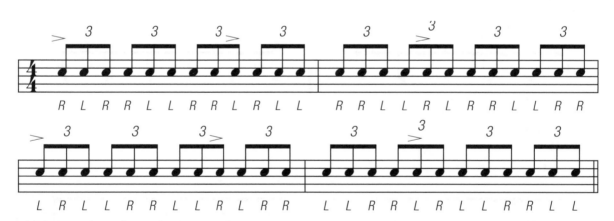

Example 23

Let's try a similar thing with the double paradiddle, but instead we'll play it as 16th notes over two bars but adding a paradiddle to turn it around, as shown in Example 24.

Example 24

Inverted Stickings

'The sticking is everything.' *Steve Gadd*

By rearranging the sticking of some of the previous rudiments, we can create some really useful alternative stickings. For example, if you take the basic paradiddle sticking, there are three other permutations hiding in there – as shown in Example 25 – that apply well to funky, broken-time playing that you might have heard used by David Garibaldi.

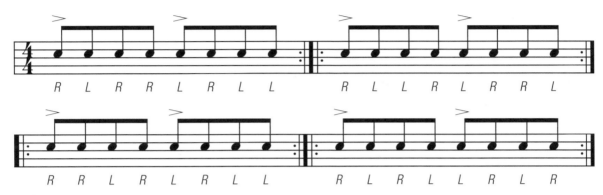

Example 25

Inverting the paradiddle-diddle-diddle also works well, as shown in Example 26, and Example 27 demonstrates a couple of Steve Gadd-inspired applications. These examples are written below as 16th notes but will probably apply better when played as 32nd notes.

Example 26

Example 27

Another useful alternative sticking can be found in the paradiddle-diddle, shown in Example 28. If you split this new sticking (often referred to as the six-stroke roll) in half to give two RLL or RRL stickings, they can be used to create a very fluid-sounding phrasing tool. Play RLL when you see a quarter note and RRL when you see an upbeat eighth note. Also check out the downbeat/upbeat exercise in Example 29. Try working through Reading Text A (page 47) in the same way. Also, be sure to try the orchestration ideas using the toms and cymbals.

Example 28

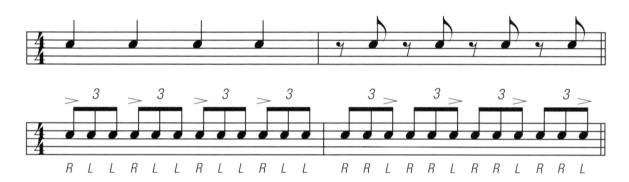

Example 29

A great way to work on all of the paradiddle stickings is to take the phrase used in Example 24 but to play the same idea over one bar. We can do this by playing groups of six, six and four. If we do this, the half-paradiddle at the end of the phrase forces the sticking to reverse on repeat, enabling both hands to be worked on. In the example, various stickings are used in order: double paradiddle, paradiddle-diddle, RLLRLL sticking (great for developing double strokes), single strokes and, finally, the six-stroke roll. Obviously, the same tempo won't work for all of them – for example, the single strokes won't go anywhere near as quick as the paradiddle-diddle – so try working them up to speed individually. Try orchestrating the accents as before. Accents in brackets are also optional, as in Example 30).

Flams

You might have heard it said that everything played on the kit is a combination of doubles, singles and flams, so it would seem appropriate to delve into some flam possibilities. To begin with, let's take a look at four important hand-to-hand flam figures: the flam, flam taps, flam accents and flam paradiddles (or flam-a-diddles, as they're sometimes called). As you'll see, all of these figures move from hand to hand, with an extra note added in each one. I've notated each hand part for each exercise (Example 31). Here are a couple of four-bar exercises that combine the previous figures. Try applying our same orchestration ideas to accented notes (Example 32). You could also try playing hand-to-hand flams in situations where you might normally play single

Example 30

strokes on the snare. (Steve Smith does this extremely well by creating a much thicker-sounding effect.)

Using these stickings is not the only way to place accents within phrases. There are certain situations where flamming accents within single strokes can also work well. Example 33 shows the single figures we looked at with the single and double strokes. Recognise the single-accented groups of three? Yes, it's the flam accent. Try working through the permutation exercises in Example 8 in the same way. Here are the first two measures of the second exercise

shown with the accents now flammed. Finally, we can take some reading text and interpret the notes as flammed accents within single strokes (Example 34).

Example 35 shows the same four measures of reading text as used in Examples 10 and 13 as flammed accents within single-stroke 16th notes and eighth-note triplets respectively.

Another flam rudiment that applies well to the drum kit is the Swiss Army triplet, shown in Example 36. Gary Novak uses these quite spectacularly, but a lot of the time he plays a left-hand flam on the first note. This

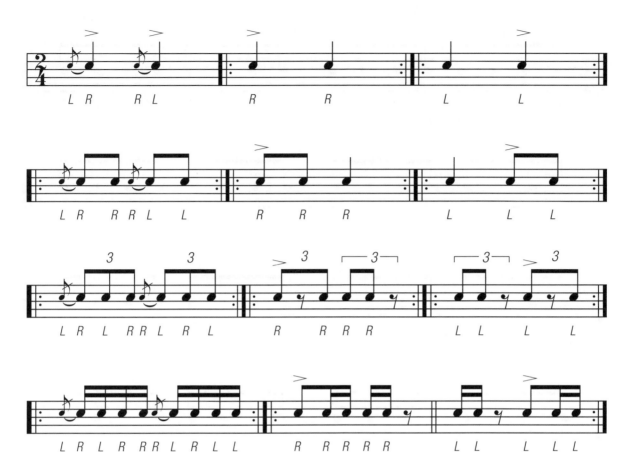

Example 31

creates a much fatter sound when played between the floor tom and snare, for instance (Example 37a). He also plays them between the ride and snare, but without flamming the first note (Example 37b). Another nice-sounding variation is to move the left hand between the toms and snare with the toms played on the first note and the snare on the third partial of the triplet (Example 37c). You can also double the right-hand stroke that comes back to the snare on the second partial of the triplet (Examples 38a, 38b, 38c). And, by adding another note in the left hand you can create a group of four (Example 39), which enables more interesting phrasing ideas to be created. Try applying some of the ideas used in Examples 37 and 38 to Examples 40a and 40b.

Ratamacues

In its basic form, the ratamacue might seem an unlikely

candidate for contemporary drum-set applications, but with a little adjustment you have what's sometimes referred to in drumming circles as the Steve Gadd ratamacue. By simply playing the first note on the bass drum and evenly spacing the dragged left-hand notes, you get six evenly spaced notes which, with the tom orchestration, seem to fall into the bass drum on beat 1 (Example 41). This basic figure can also be played several different ways (Example 42) and when combined with the six-stroke roll concept discussed earlier creates a very slick phrasing idea.

As mentioned earlier, the rudiments and concepts presented here are by no means a conclusive list of rudiments but rather a study of those that can be applied directly to the drum kit. If you wish to explore this kind of material further, you could do worse than to check out Charlie Wilcoxen's *Rudimental Swing Solos* or, for more phrasing ideas, Jim Blackley's

Example 32

Syncopated Rolls For The Modern Drummer. There is the danger of getting lost completely down the unlit path that is practising endless combinations of rudiments which have more to do with the drum corps than the drum kit, but these two books have a positive musical flow and application that makes them enjoyable and useful regardless of what style of music you play.

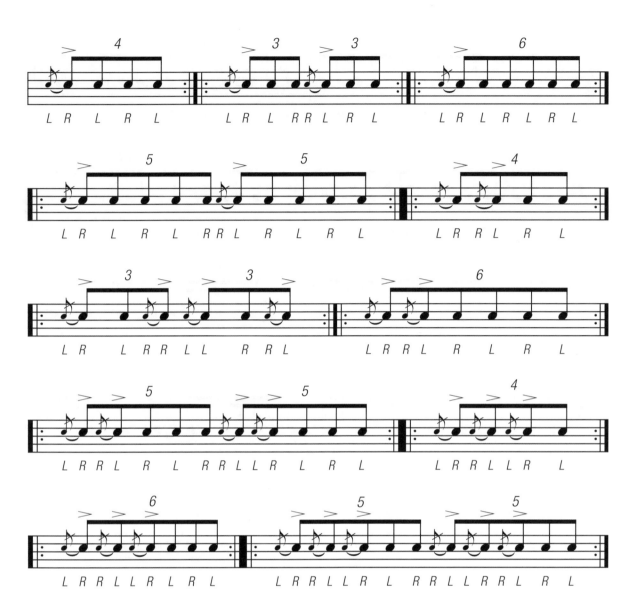

Example 33

Example 34

Example 35

Example 36

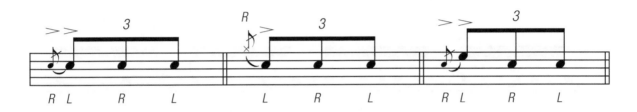

Example 37a   **Example 37b**   **Example 37c**

Example 38a   **Example 38b**   **Example 38c**

Example 39

Example 40a

Example 40b

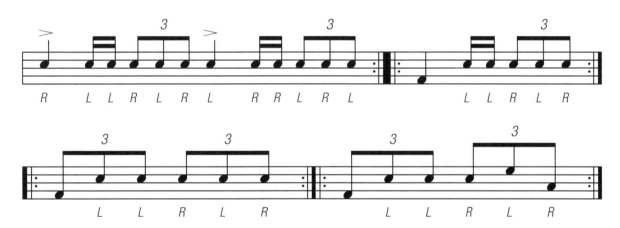

Example 41

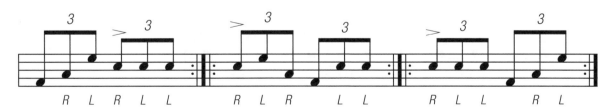

Example 42

4 TIME PLAYING

Even if you've no desire to become a first-call session musician, having the ability to play different styles of music convincingly will make you a better all-round musician. It will also increase your vocabulary and develop your co-ordination. This chapter focuses on developing the independence, sound and feel required to play these styles well.

Most of the time when playing grooves they're based around an ostinato pattern played in the right hand. An ostinato is simply a pattern that repeats, so, for example, even if we play a simple groove with eighth notes in the right hand and 2 and 4 on the snare, regardless of what the bass drum does our hands are playing an ostinato. Let's begin with this basic eighth-note time feel while working

through the eighth and 16th-note reading text on the bass drum. This approach helps to develop real flexibility with the bass drum and helps move away from playing 'beats', enabling the music to dictate the kick-drum pattern. (If playing through the reading text is proving difficult, check out the CD, on which you'll find each of the four reading texts played on the snare to a click.)

Here's the basic hand pattern, shown along with the first four measures of Reading Texts A, B and D respectively. Once you can play the examples, work through the remaining reading texts (A, B, D – we'll get to C in a moment). Don't worry if you can't play straight down the whole page; work on one bar at a time if necessary.

Example 1a

Reading Text A (bars 1-4)

Reading Text A (full score)

Example 1b

Reading Text B (bars 1-4)

Reading Text B (full score)

Example 1d

Reading Text D (bars 1-4)

Reading Text D (full score)

The next step is four-way coordination. If you've never spent time getting the left foot moving on the hi-hat, this is going to be a challenge, but it really is worth the effort. I can recall working through this material and having to take each bass-drum figure individually and work out how it lined up with the left-foot part. I also hear a lot of students saying that they're unable to maintain their balance, especially when playing the left foot heel-up, which can be attributed to posture and sitting too far back on the stool, not allowing the legs freedom to move. Below are the three time patterns, along with all of the basic 16th-note based figures. (Notice that in Example 2 the right hand has moved from the hi-hat to the ride cymbal.) These figures are included as a reference for when you're working through the reading texts and encountering individual figures which cause you problems.

Once you're familiar with Example 2, take a look at the first four measures of Reading Text C (page 54) and our three new time patterns: Examples 3a, 3b and 3c.

Example 2

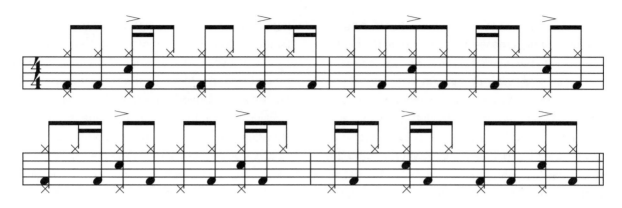

Example 3a

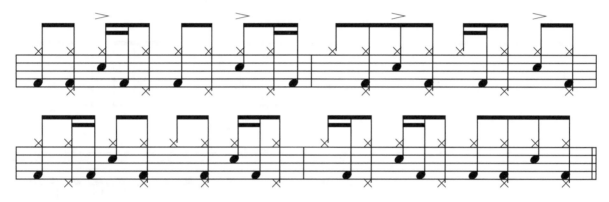

Example 3b

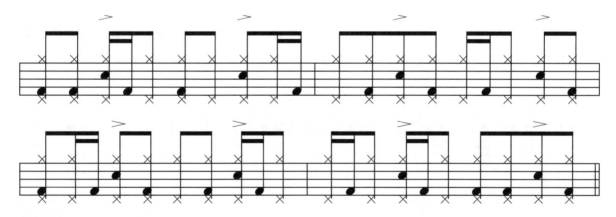

Example 3c

As I said, this is tricky stuff, but the possibilities that it gives your drumming are great. For example, if you're able to splash the hi-hat, upbeat eighths create a great counterpoint to quarter-note accents on the cymbal. Constant eighth notes can also give the impression of a shaker being added to the groove – or a tambourine, if you fit one to the hi-hat stand. And if you open and close the hats with the left foot on either quarter-notes or upbeat eighths, it sounds like you've grown another arm! In fact, just splashing quarter notes when you move off the hi-hat can sound really effective and help maintain the pulse.

Here are some more time patterns to work through in the same way. This isn't by any means a list of all the possible time-playing ostinatos but rather a run-down of some of the most commonly used examples. Don't worry, they can all be played along with the three left-foot hi-hat figures. Try not to be deterred by the time you think it will take you to master these because, to be honest, you'll probably find that, as you work your way through each one, co-ordination will begin to feel more and more natural.

Be sure to maintain the accents in the right hand as you work through the bass drum reading. You could also try the different left-foot patterns, keeping your right hand on the hi-hat. (Keeping your left heel down on the footplate should give you some interesting open and closed hi-hat grooves.) Another fun way to practise the various right-hand patterns is to pick a nice-sounding kick-and-snare pattern and, starting with eighth notes with the right hand, move through the various ostinatos (Example 4).

Whilst playing '2 and 4' can work well, there are times when an alternative snare placement can sound better. For example, if we take the basic groove in Example 5a, we could replace the bass drum on the fourth 16th note of 1 with the snare drum (Example 5b) or alternatively on the 'and' of 2 (Example 5c).

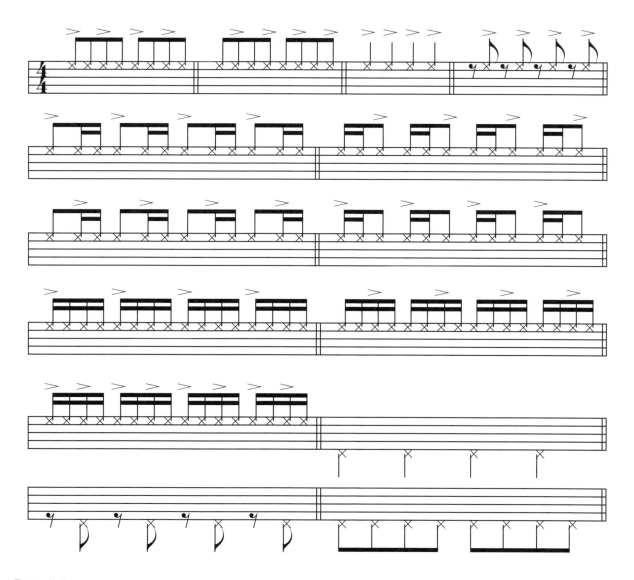

Example 4

Example 5a   **Example 5b**   **Example 5c**

Reading Text C (full score)

Examples 6a–h show some more kick/snare grooves that feature some interesting snare placements. They're written without an ostinato in the right hand and are to be practised with any or all of the previous examples. When working through these figures, try to maintain the correct accent pattern in the right hand so that the flow of notes remains unaffected by where the backbeat is falling.

Example 6a　　　　　　　　　　　**Example 6b**

Example 6c　　　　　　　　　　　**Example 6d**

Example 6e　　　　　　　　　　　**Example 6f**

Example 6g　　　　　　　　　　　**Example 6h**

Another important 16th-note time feel is hand-to-hand 16ths. Most of us, I'm sure have used the basic RLRL feel at some point but there are some subtle changes that can create some great sounding variations. Example 7a shows first the basic feel with the right hand moving from hi-hat to snare on 2 and 4. You could try playing an accent on all four quarter notes with all other notes played unaccented (Example 7b). In louder situations you could play the hats slightly open and all at the same dynamic (Example 7c). Whilst on the subject of dynamics, accenting the first and fourth 16th of each beat can create a nice feel regardless of the bass drum pattern (Example 7d). And, finally, here's a great variation I first heard played by Steve Gadd. It involves playing 2 and 4 and the 16th before and after it in the left hand on the hi-hat. This method eliminates the 'drop-out' on the hi-hat on 2 and 4 where the right hand moves across to the snare and it also enables you to open the hi-hat on two and four (Example 7e). Our final variation is a little different to the previous examples in that although hand-to-hand 16ths are used, the left hand remains on the snare. At a recent drum clinic first-call session drummer JR Robinson said that this groove was the current groove of choice on a lot of recent sessions. For it be effective try to keep the left hand as quiet as possible on the ghosted notes (Example 7f). Once comfortable with all of these variations you could also try working through the reading text in the same way as the previous examples.

Example 7a

Example 7b

Example 7c

Example 7d

R L R L L L L R L R L R L L L L R L

Example 7e

R L R L etc

Example 7f

Paradiddles, Ghosting And Broken-Time Playing

Up to now, we've looked at playing an ostinato in the right hand combined with a backbeat and some bass-drum variations. Now we're going to look at a more broken approach to playing time where the hands play time based around stickings. This is similar to linear playing, where no two sounds fall together, but the restriction implied in that seems a little odd to me, so here we're going to use the four paradiddle stickings we looked at earlier. Personally, I think they're the best way of developing consistent ghosting, as hidden within them are all of the essential ghosting moves.

Firstly, let's play them as 16th notes between the hi-hat and snare drum, with the kick drum on 1 and 3. In all of these exercises, the right hand should remain on the hi-hat and the left on the snare. Try playing all of the hi-hat accents with the shoulder of the stick on the edge and unaccented notes on top. Meanwhile, on the snare, play all accents as rimshots with all unaccented beats played as quietly as possible just off centre to thin the sound out even more. It can't be over-stressed just how quiet the left hand needs to be in order to make this work, so try to keep the left-hand ghost notes down to about half an inch, as shown in Examples 1a, 1b, 1c and 1d.

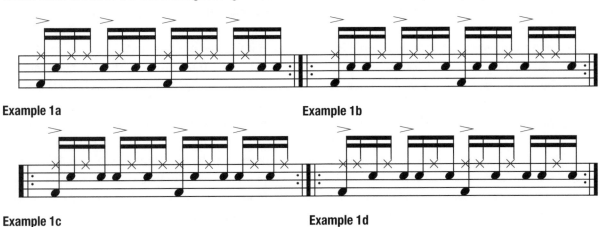

Example 1a

Example 1b

Example 1c

Example 1d

As you can see, the Examples 1c and 1d are the most difficult, both requiring the ability to play unaccented notes directly before or after an accent. It really takes some work to develop the right sound because the accent needs to be played at the same volume as your regular backbeat volume.

When playing the ghosted note before the accent, you need to develop a snap-back into the hand, whereas when ghosting after the accent the art of

achieving the desired effect lies in killing the stick dead immediately after playing the accent.

Although you might not want to use the paradiddles as regular grooves, there are still some funky moves hidden with their different stickings. Examples 2a–2d show four variations that each use the same basic sticking; only the bass drum pattern and accent placement has changed. Notes in parenthesis can be safely ignored.

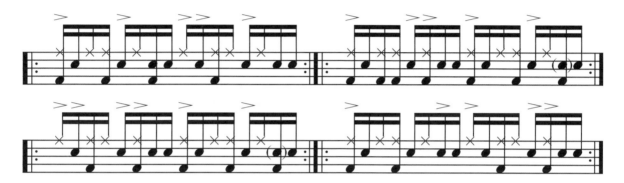

Example 2a

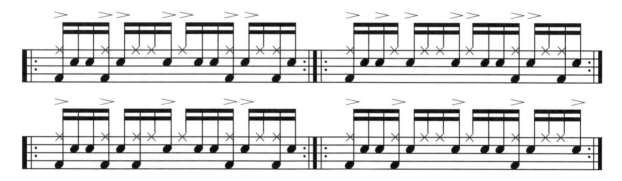

Example 2b

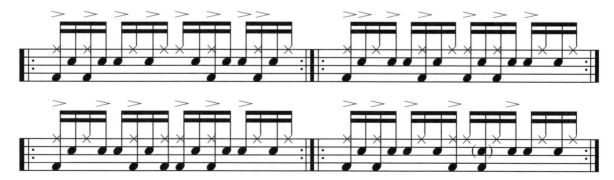

Example 2c

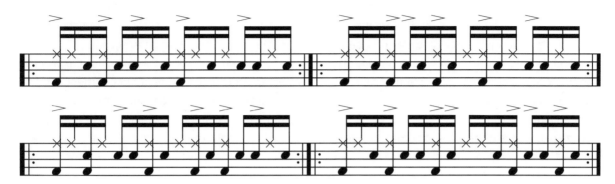

Example 2d

Another way of getting fluent with these paradiddles is to try choosing one of the four stickings and working through the reading text on the bass drum. Example 3 shows the basic paradiddle played along with the second line of Reading Text D (page 50).

For more inspiration on these types of grooves, you could do worse than check out David Garibaldi's books, videos and playing. He wrote the book on this subject (literally, check out *Future Sounds*), and as hip and fresh as some of it sounds, it can be heard in his playing way back in the early '70s with Tower Of Power. Another master of this broken-time playing is Zack Danziger, whose playing on guitarist Wayne Krantz's *2 Drink Minimum* is amazing.

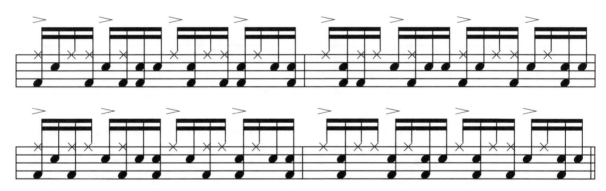

Example 3

We can also apply ghost notes to ostinato grooves, and below (Examples 4a–4d) are presented four of the most useful grooves for developing your ghosting ability. These should be practised really slowly at first, paying attention to internal dynamics and making sure that all of the 16th notes flow evenly.

Example 4a

Example 4b

Example 4c

Example 4d

Notice how none of the examples includes accents on the right hand. This is because they should be practised with accents on both downbeats and upbeats. The final example is a little different, insomuch as the snare and bass drum make up constant 16th notes. This means that you can play any of the right-hand ostinatos over the top. You can also create some funky-sounding variations by accenting some of the left-hand notes that fall on the 'and' of a group of four (Example 5). Also try going back to the alternative snare-placement exercises, filling in all of the spaces with ghost notes in the left hand. Example 6a shows a pattern with eighth notes in the right hand, while 6b shows an eighth/two-16th-note pattern.

Example 5

Example 6a   **Example 6b**

Swing Playing

These days, most drummers grow up playing some form of pop and rock music, and when confronted with the prospect of playing a jazz tune or even something in a triplet or swung-eighth-note timing feel like a fish out of water. Working through the single, double and six-stroke roll exercises in Chapter 3, 'Rudiments', will help you to get your ideas flowing in a swing feel, but what about playing time? When teaching at the ACM, I encounter quite a few drummers who need help with their jazz playing. When I ask them to tell me which area of their playing needs work, they'll often respond with answers like, 'I just don't know how to put it all together.' My response is usually, 'Well, how much jazz are you playing or listening to?' The answer often ranges from 'not much' to 'none'. It seems that a lot of players are working on their jazz playing from books and videos, perhaps not even sure why they're working on it other than that they've heard Dave Weckl and Vinnie do it, but they're not allowing the music to shape their development. In other words, you need to know why you're playing what it is you're playing, and this can really come only from listening to and playing music, regardless of the style.

Another type of student I often encounter are those who think jazz or swing playing has no part in the kind of drummer they want to be. At around this point, I like to get them to play a blues shuffle, a hip-hop groove, or maybe Jeff Porcaro's legendary groove from 'Rosanna'. By now the point is usually made: how can you play these time feels and have them feel good without an understanding of jazz time playing?

It would be silly of us both to assume that in the limited space we have here that I can turn you into the next Tony Williams, so instead I've presented a variety of ways of developing swing-time playing which should be enough to get even the most ardent rocker playing along to a few jazz standards.

Let's begin with the essence of swing-time playing, the quarter-note pulse, but looking first at the feet. Example 1 below shows one of the most important foot ostinatos (others might include the samba, tumbao and baiao in the Latin section) and it involves playing quarter notes with the right foot and 2 and 4 with the left. To do this, the right foot is going to 'feather' the bass drum. This involves playing heel-down and allowing the beater to rebound off the head. It should be done very lightly so that it's felt and not heard. The hi-hat is then played with a rocking motion so that the heel comes down on 1 and 3 and the toe comes down on 2 and 4, giving a closed-hi-hat sound. By using this motion in the left foot, although you hear the hi-hat only on beats 2 and 4, both feet are moving on quarter notes. Spend some time getting this to feel smooth and locked together.

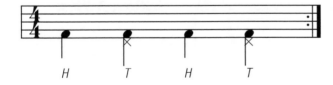

Example 1

The next three steps involve adding quarter notes on the cymbal with the right hand, as shown in Example 2. Try playing this midway between the bell and the edge (too near the bell sounds thin and staccato and too near the edge sounds washy). The left hand is then added, lightly playing the third partial of the triplet, the *skip note*. Once comfortable, add the second partial with a slight accent on the third. Try getting this to flow at a wide variety of tempos, from 40bpm up to 200bpm.

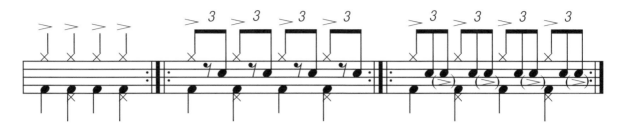

Example 2

Next we'll try a similar thing with the shuffle. Now the right hand is playing the quarter note and skip note combined (Example 3), and in order for this to feel right the skip note should be played more quietly than the quarter note. The left hand then fills in the

trip, the skip note and, finally, both. Again, when playing both, try to emphasise the skip note in the left hand. This is a tricky piece of co-ordination, so take your time and be sure to get it happening from 40bpm upwards.

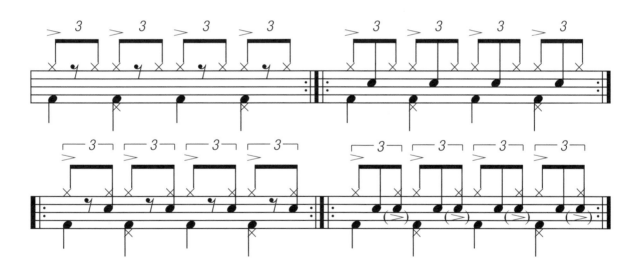

Example 3

Finally, do the same with the jazz-ride pattern shown in Example 4. This could be regarded as a combination of the quarter-note pulse and the shuffle (quarter notes on 1 and 3 and the shuffle on 2 and 4). Again make

sure that the quarter-note pulse can still be heard clearly. It's shown with some other left-hand figures designed to help develop some independence between the hands.

Example 4

Now let's try working through some reading text, reading the figures in the left hand. Let's begin with Reading Text A (page 47), which we're going to interpret here with a swing feel. Basically, this involves simply playing all upbeat eighth notes on the third partial of the triplet. So if, for example, you took the second bar on the third line, it would go from looking like Example 5a to Example 5b. It's really that simple. All that needs to be remembered is that nothing will fall on the middle partial of the triplet (the trip). With this in mind, here are the last four measures of Reading Text A played in the left hand, along with the jazz-time feel (Example 6).

Example 5a   **Example 5b**

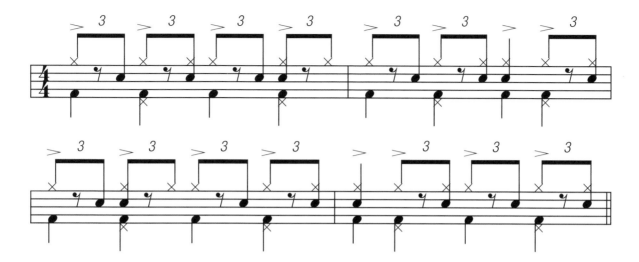

Example 6

Next try the same text but reading it on the bass drum. Try playing the left hand as a cross-stick on 4. You might want to start by getting the second measure feeling good first as this, along with the quarter note, is the basis for all 16 measures. As the bass drum is also now part of the comping (accompaniment), it should be played louder than when feathered. Example 7 shows the first four measures written in full.

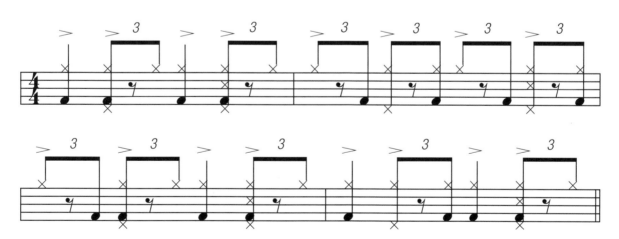

Example 7

Now, using the same text, try playing the figures on the snare with the bass drum filling in all of the swung-eighth spaces. Here's the first line written that way (Example 8).

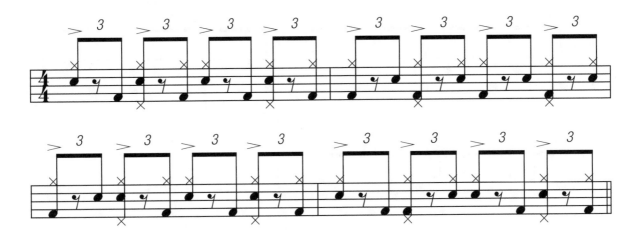

Example 8

The next step of this development process involves breaking away from the jazz ride pattern. Now it's the right hand and bass drum that play the figure with the left hand filling in all of the swung eighth notes. Again, here's the first line played in this way (Example 9).

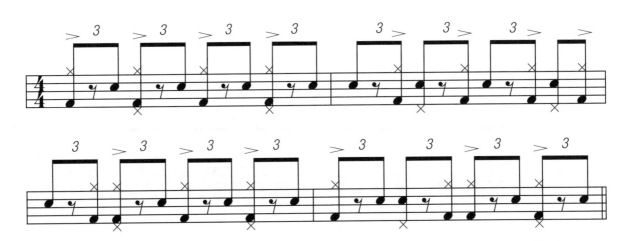

Example 9

Steve Gadd and Elvin Jones, to name just two, use this final 'right-hand lead' phrasing idea extensively. As with the previous idea, it involves playing the figure with the right hand and bass drum, but now the left hand fills in eighth-note triplets. This is all well and good until you encounter more than a quarter-note rest, like that between the first two measures of Reading Text A, for example. Here, to avoid having to play four consecutive left-hand notes, the right hand plays the downbeat on the second measure as a pick-up note, as shown in Example 10. This can be played on either the snare drum or the cymbal.

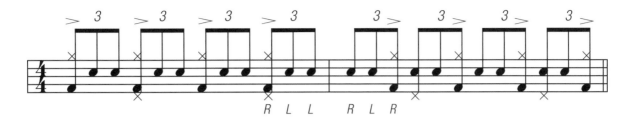

Example 10

Example 11 shows the last four measures of Reading Text A played in this way.

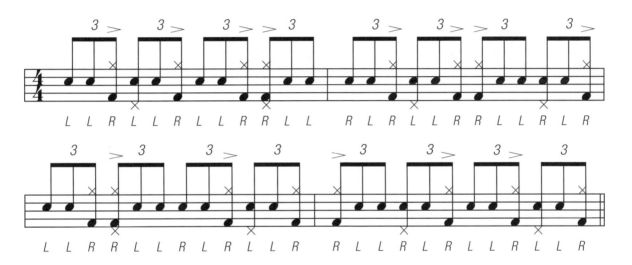

Example 11

Another frequently used phrasing idea when playing jazz time is changing up the ride cymbal pattern. This is done by adding or subtracting quarter notes. In the first example below, a quarter note is taken from beat 4 of bar 1, giving the impression that a bar of three has been played. In Example 12b, a quarter note is added on beat 1 of bar two, giving the impression that a bar of five has been played. We can also do this so that groups of swung eighths are played together. Once comfortable with these three examples, try adding the snare on skip notes, as in Examples 12a, 12b, 12c.

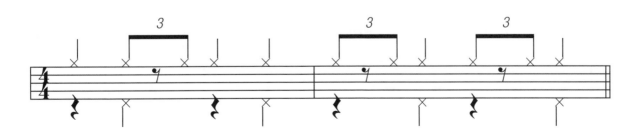

Example 12a

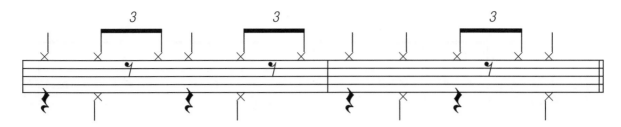

Example 12b

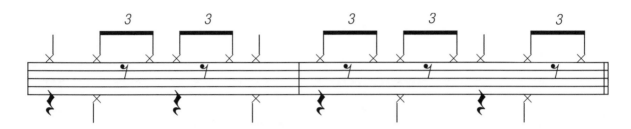

Example 12c

When playing jazz, you can sometimes be required to play tempos as quick as 400bpm! It takes a lot of work to be able to play at this sort of speed with any finesse, but the most important thing to develop is the 'flattened-out' ride pattern. At tempos of around 280–300bpm, the ride pattern loses its swing feel and is played straight. If you try to maintain the swing at these speeds, it can make the time feel uncomfortable. In fact, players such as Tony Williams would often flatten out the feel at even slower tempos. Actually, Tony Williams was a master of up-tempo playing, with a seemingly endless supply of comping, phrasing and soloing ideas.

One exercise you use to develop the basic feel is to set the click to 150bpm and, after playing four bars of time, switch to double time for eight bars. Now the click will be playing on 1 and 3. In fact, try getting the bass drum to do the same – play quarter notes at 150bpm, then switch to half notes at 300, as shown in Example 13. Playing the bass drum on 1 and 3 at quick tempos can seem odd at first, but at a lesson I had with John Riley he said that it puts a smile on the bass player's face as everything feels more grounded. As you get more comfortable at the quicker tempo, try doubling the lengths: 8 bars to 16, 16 bars to 32 and so on. Changing up the ride pattern can also help as, by adding a few quarter-notes here and there, it can give your arm a small but much-needed rest.

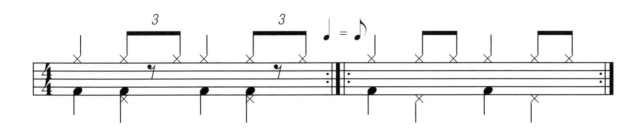

Example 13

Brush Playing

How could we look at swing playing without looking at brush playing? Unfortunately, playing with brushes seems to be becoming a lost art these days. When I'm teaching and I ask students to bring in their brushes, most young drummers admit to not even owning a pair. This is a shame, as playing with brushes gives you an opportunity to play with subtlety and with a smooth legato feel – quite the opposite of the pounding 2-and-4 backbeat. If you haven't spent much time playing with brushes, get accustomed to the different balances, weights and response by working through the same sort of exercises that you might work on with sticks (singles, doubles, paradiddles and so on).

Now let's try to play some basic jazz time on the snare. When playing brushes, it's not uncommon for drummers to turn off the snares. This allows more of the intricacies to be heard and can also work well during bass solos, where buzzing snares can be a real distraction. The first thing to realise when playing jazz time on the snare is that the left hand must play in time and not simply go round and round in circles on its own accord. When doing, this try to keep your left hand low so that the brush is almost flat to the drum. This helps to create a nice smooth sound, as opposed to having the tip of the brush digging into the head. In the first medium-tempo example below on the next page, the

right hand is playing the jazz ride pattern with the quarter-notes moving between the 4 o'clock and 11 o'clock positions, with the 'and' of the 2 and 4 played at four o-clock. When playing this – and any time pattern in the right hand – try stopping the brush just short of the drum, allowing the tip to flick down onto the head. This creates a nice clear note instead of simply playing the brush into the drum. The left hand now plays a clockwise circular motion. The hands should cross on 2 and 4 and at this point apply a little pressure with the left hand to emphasise the 2 and 4. A nice-sounding alternative seen in the second exercise is to leave the right brush on the head as it sweeps from 1 to 2 and from 3 to 4. Again the hands still cross on 2 and 4 and the left hand should still emphasise 2 and 4 (medium-tempo diagram).

Along with the sweeping sound and the tap sounds looked at so far, there is another useful sound to be addressed. This is the brush equivalent of a rimshot and is used for accenting. To do this, whip the brush down onto the head with the shoulder (the point where the brushes leave the main body of the brush), with the tip hitting the head at the same time. This should be practised using both hands. Once you're comfortable doing this, try the following accenting exercises In Example 1. These should be practised with either hand playing the accent. Try playing one bar of time and then one of the exercises.

Example 1

The patterns looked at so far will work well at most medium tempos, but at slower ballad tempos we need to take up more of the space between the notes. To do this, the left hand now plays a clockwise quarter-note

pulse, with the slight emphasis on the quarter note. The right hand has a few options: it can simply play the same quarter-note pulse but anti-clockwise (this pattern almost always sounds great when used in a ballad), or it can

Medium Tempos

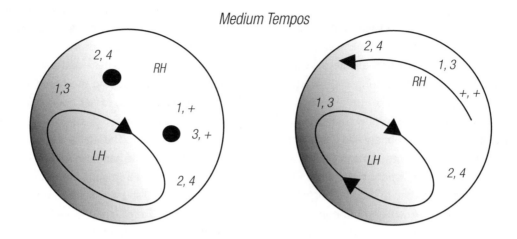

Ballads

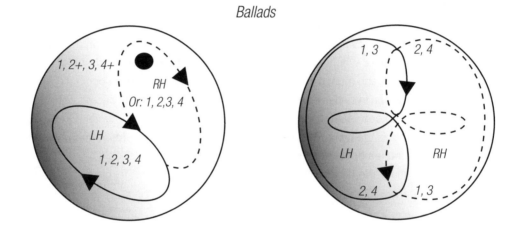

Up Tempos

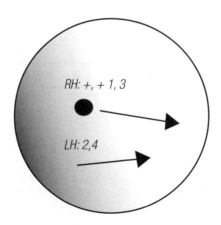

Brush-playing diagrams

play either the jazz ride pattern or straight eighths, depending on the subdivision of the tune.

Another pattern similar to the first ballad pattern, with both hands playing the quarter note, is the figure-of-eight pattern. This actually looks more difficult than it is. Basically, think of the drum head as though it's divided into quarters. Each hand begins playing the quarter-note pulse in opposite corners and then sweeps up or down to the quarter of the drum above or below it. This is then repeated so that each hand is playing the pulse while moving up and down, but also while moving in opposite directions. As you get more comfortable, you can begin to sweep the top hand over the bottom to create an even more intense sweeping sound, shown in the ballad diagram on the previous page.

At the opposite end of the metronome are the up-tempo patterns, shown on the previous page. As we know, at speeds around and above 300bpm the swing feel flattens out. At this point it becomes impossible to play the medium-tempo brush patterns, so now the pattern is broken up between the hands, with the right hand playing 1, the 'and' of 2, 3 and the 'and' of 4, while the left plays 2 and 4. When combined and played up to speed, this actually sounds like the regular pattern.

When playing with brushes, it can sound nice if you incorporate the hi-hat (the sound of which blends well with the brushes) into comping and soloing ideas. Example 2 below shows some of my favourites. In the first four exercises, the right hand, although written on the ride cymbal, is played on the snare as normal.

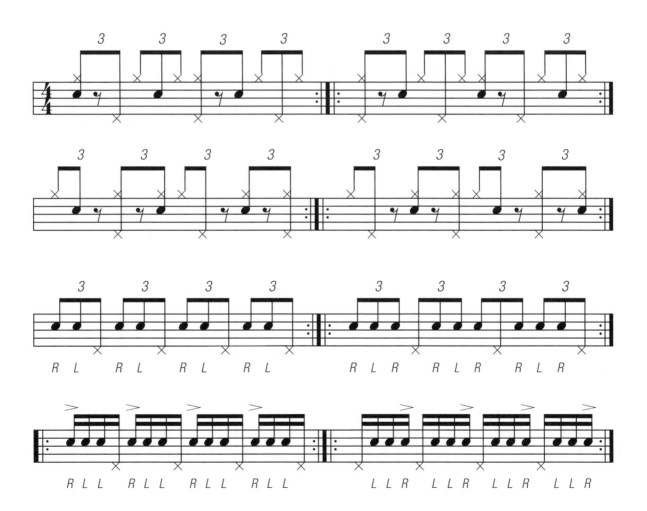

Example 2

Example 2 (continued)

As well as being used in jazz, brushes can also be used in pop and rock situations to great effect. Along with hot-rod-type sticks, they can be used to play regular grooves, but they create a much different atmosphere. For example, simply by using brushes and moving the right hand from the hi-hat to the snare or floor tom, a regular rock or pop groove can start to sound like something very different.

Shuffles

Laying down a good shuffle groove is a pre-requisite for any drummer. There are many variations of the shuffle groove – jazz, blues, rock – and whether or not the bass player is walking (playing quarter notes), but the thing that prevails through all of them is the feel. The shuffle is based around swung eighth notes but at mid tempos, and this applies to jazz time playing as

well – the skip note tends to creep closer to the quarter note. To illustrate the point, work through the following two exercises (Example 1). Once you can play each exercise comfortably, try alternating between one bar of each. Then, while doing this, move your left hand onto your leg so that only the right hand can be heard. What you should hear is the subtle movement of the skip note to the fourth 16th note of the beat. In reality, it's not quite as cut and dried as this and lies somewhere between the two – in the cracks, as it were – but it should illustrate the elusive shuffle feel. Try applying the same approach to the following grooves, which are all shuffle grooves that will work in various situations. Those written with the hi-hat on 2 and 4 can be played with the hi-hats on all four quarter notes, especially in blues and rock situations. The hi-hat can also be splashed in all exercises (Example 2).

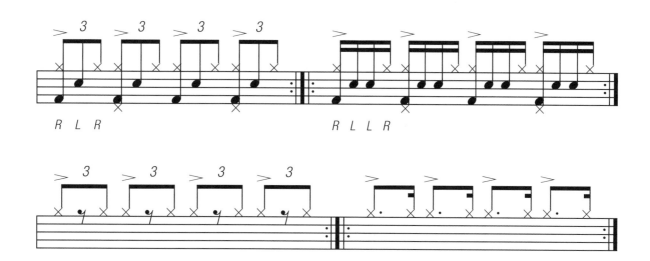

Example 1

Example 2

The next set of exercises, in Example 3, are more rock or pop shuffle grooves where the middle partial of the triplet has been added as a ghost note on the snare.

These eighth-note-triplet grooves will work well in situations where the bass player is playing something other than a walking line.

Example 3

One commonly used accent figure within shuffle feels is hitting the 'and' of 2 or 4, and when playing the shuffles shown in the first set of exercises this is easy as you can simply keep the feet playing quarter notes and hit the figure with the cymbal and snare. However, with the last set of exercises the feel is based around constant eighth-note-triplets, so the figure can be difficult to play smoothly. Examples 4 and 5 show you how to play this figure and maintain the eight-note-triplet feel, with Example 4 shown off the hi-hat and 5 off the hi-tom.

Example 4

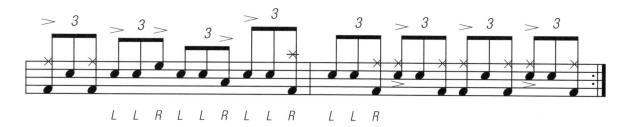

L L R L L R L L R   L L R

Example 5

Half Time Shuffles

Arguably one of the most talked-about grooves in drumming (perhaps joint first with Steve Gadd's '50 Ways To Leave Your Lover') is the groove that the great drummer Jeff Porcaro played on the Toto track 'Rosanna'. It consisted of a ghosted shuffle groove with a backbeat on 3 and the bass-drum pattern playing a Bo Diddley/go-go pattern. But before we reach that point, let's take a look at the basic feel. Example 1 below shows a basic half-time shuffle. Although this feel is sometimes notated this way, it's often felt as more of a swung 16th-note feel. If we double the rate up to 16th-note triplets, we get

two backbeats on 2 and 4 (Example 2). This we can interpret as 16th-note-based reading text in the same way as we did the eight-note triplet text. For example, if we were to interpret the first bar of Reading Text C (page 54) on the bass drum with our straight 16th-note pattern, it would look like Example 3. And if we were to do the same with the swung 16th-note version it would look like Example 4. So it basically works in the same way as the triplet interpretation insofar as nothing will fall in the spaces in the hi-hat pattern. Example 5 shows the first four measures of Reading Text C interpreted in exactly the same way.

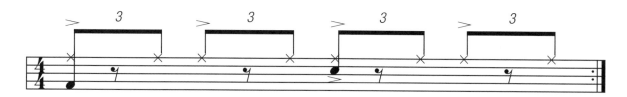

Example 1

Example 2

Example 3

Example 4

Example 5

Now we can add the ghost notes to the hi-hat pattern (Examples 6a, 6b). This can be tricky – a lot of players miss out the ghosted note after the backbeat. Remember when interpreting the reading text that nothing coincides with the ghost notes. Example 7 shows the second line of Reading Text C interpreted on the bass drum.

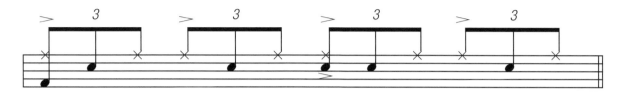

Example 6a

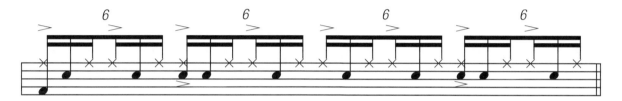

Example 6b

Example 7

Hip-Hop, Shuffle, Funk And Swing 16ths

While this half-time-shuffle stuff is all well and good at medium tempos, squeezing in all of those 16th-note triplets gets tricky when playing quicker swung 16th-note feels. The solution is to drop the subdivision from 16th-note triplets down to swung 16ths. This is where some fluidity with the jazz ride-cymbal pattern really helps, as it's the equivalent of playing jazz time in the right hand with a backbeat on 3 in the left (the only difference being that it's felt in a swung-16th-note feel). There are actually two ways of phrasing the ride: forwards or reverse. Example 1 shows a basic groove with the two different ride cymbal patterns. Filling in the ghost notes works well with the first exercise but not so well with the second (Examples 2a, 2b), where the move from ghost note to backbeat becomes difficult at quicker tempos.

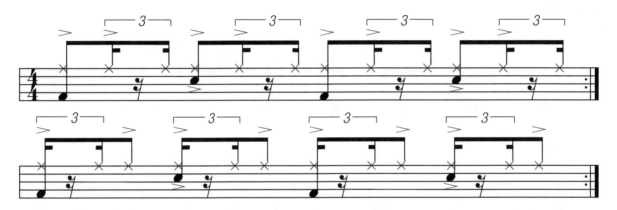

Example 1

Examples 2a

Examples 2b

You could also try stepping the hi-hat on quarter-note or upbeat eighths. This works particularly well when playing the hi-hat and creates some funky-sounding hi-hat patterns. To develop some fluidity with the bass drum along with these time feels, you could try interpreting the reading text in the same way as was done with the half-time shuffle. Example 3 shows the first four measures of Reading Text C played along with Example 2a. Usually, this sort of feel will be written on a chart as straight 16ths and called something like 'Swing 16ths', or notated at the top:

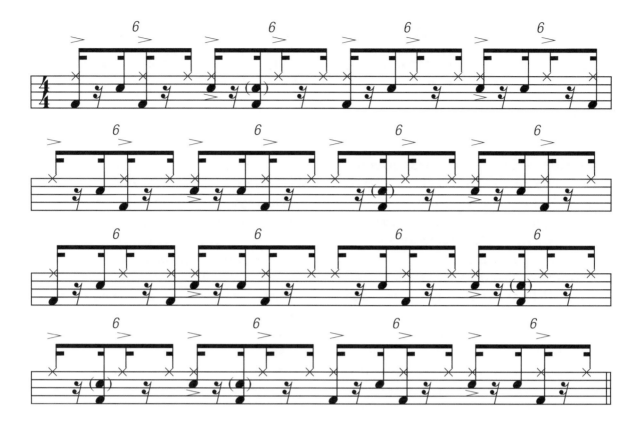

Example 3

Example 4 shows what the previous four measures would look like written this way – you must agree, it's easier to read. When playing tunes with this feel, remember to swing all 16th notes, unless you intend otherwise. Straight 16ths can work well, creating tension, but only if used sparingly.

Example 4

To create some other interesting and funky grooves, try going back to the displaced-snare exercises earlier in this chapter and work through them using these time feels. Example 5 shows what the Examples 6a and 6b of the previous section would look like when played with the time feel used in Examples 3 and 4.

Example 5

New Orleans Second Line Grooves

Another great-sounding swing (or partially swung) feel is the second-line feel. Originating from New Orleans, second-line drumming is traditionally played by two drummers, one playing the bass drum and the other the snare. They would play at funerals to celebrate the lives of the people buried. The rhythms consist of syncopated figures played back and forth between the bass drum and snare, creating swinging time feels. These figures usually consist of six notes per phrase per drum and would often be played 'between the cracks' – not straight and not swung. The basic groove is played using single strokes on the snare, but because of the swung nature of the feel it's deceptively tricky. A good way of developing this is to work through Reading Text A (page 47) in this way, as shown below in Example 1. Try playing it both straight and swung. Playing this in-the-cracks feel can be tricky at first because we're so used to our playing falling into a specific subdivision – 8ths, 16ths and so on – so when you first begin you'll probably keep falling one way or the other, with swung eighths to one side and straight eighths the other. Eventually you'll begin to find a strange – but undeniably funky – line somewhere between the two.

Another great development exercise would be to add the hi-hat on 2 and 4 and add the bass-drum filling in all of the swung eighths between the snare accents, as shown in Example 2.

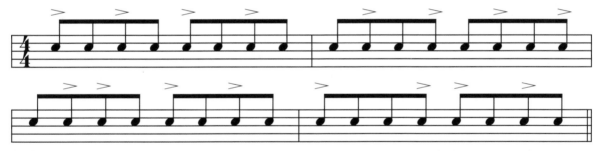

Example 1

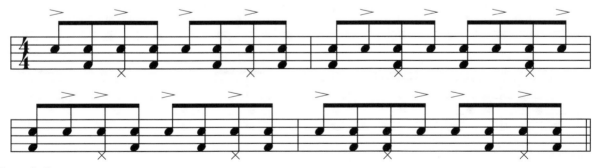

Example 2

Now you've developed some co-ordination, let's take a look at a basic second-line groove. Example 3a shows a typical second-line groove made up of six notes/accents on the bass drum and snare. If we remove all the other notes, we get the figure shown in Example 3b and we can create seven more figures by displacing this initial figure by one quarter-note to the right, as in Example 4. These all swing in their own way.

Example 3a

Example 3b

Example 4

All of these figures can also be played along with the jazz ride pattern or the shuffle pattern (as in Examples 5a and 5b), where they make great comp exercises as well as great time feels. When playing them with the shuffle pattern, you could try adding ghost notes with the left hand so that the right foot and left hand play continuous swung eighths. With some dynamics added to the left hand, this makes for great funk grooves, such as Example 6. The New Orleans band The Meters are masters of combining the second-line feel with funk, and drummer Joseph 'Zigaboo' Modeleste makes it sound so easy

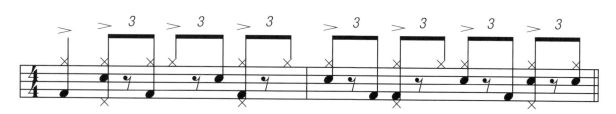

Example 5a

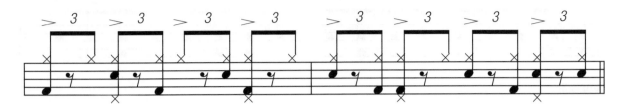

Example 5b

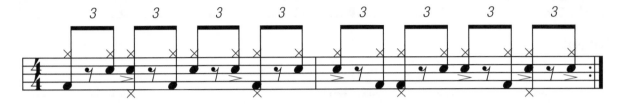

Example 6

Odd Times

Playing in odd time signatures can be a challenge as well as a fun alternative to the regular 2-and-4 backbeat. Unfortunately, a lot of drummers get scared if the tune they're trying to play isn't in the relative comfort of 4/4, or perhaps 6/8, and that's probably because if it's in 7/8 (one eighth note less than 4/4) they're counting eighth notes (1, 2, 3, 4, 5, 6, 7, 1, 2, 3, 4, 5, 6, 7 and so on). Feeling the odd time this way not only restricts your ability to phrase – after all, you don't count 4/4 as 1, 2, 3, 4, 5, 6, 7, 8, 1, 2, 3, 4, 5, 6, 7, 8 – but it also forces you into beat 1 of every measure, often resulting in a heavy downbeat whether the music needs it or not.

A far easier way to feel odd times is to find out where the rhythm pivots. In other words, most tunes in 7/8 aren't made up of seven evenly spaced eighth notes; there's more likely to be a pulse within it that's easier to play to. When playing 4/4, the chances are that you're feeling the quarter notes, and when playing odd times it can be much easier almost to step back

and do the same. This means that we can now count our bar of 7/8 as 1, 2, 3 'an', 1, 2, 3 'an'. This enables us to see the bigger picture and gives us more space to breathe. Examples 1a–1c below illustrate ways of playing 5/8 and 9/8. (On the CD I count 9/8 as 1, 2, 3, 4, 1, 2, 3, 4, 5 – it seems easier than counting to nine.)

One of the best ways of becoming fluent in these time signatures is to program these rhythms into a drum machine or sing them in your head and play around with them. The first few times you might trip up and lose '1', but after a while it should start to feel natural. I once read an interview with Vinnie Colaiuta – a master of odd time signatures – who said that when he lived at home he'd sit playing a specific time signature for 45 minutes at a time. While this might sound like hard work, you need only think of how much time you've spent playing 4/4 to appreciate why there might be an imbalance in your ability to play in different time signatures.

Examples 2a, 2b and 2c show how the pulse in the previous examples can be outlined in a groove to make even the most basic pattern feel more comfortable.

Example 1a   **Example 1b**   **Example 1c**

Example 2a

Example 2b

Example 2c

Now that you've found a way of making these odd times feel smoother, you can combine it with another way of making time playing feel even smoother still. Vinnie gets another mention here because he used this approach on several of the odd-time tunes he played with Sting. If you take a basic groove in 7/8 and apply some accents in the right hand, you'll hear that tendency to fall into beat 1. Now, if you carry the accents over the bar line where they resolve, after two measures you get a downbeat accent in the first measure and an upbeat accent in the second. This has the effect of putting the right hand in 7/4, but again it takes another step back, enabling you to see an even bigger picture, thus making the groove feel even more comfortable (Examples 3a, 3b). Examples 4a and 4b show the same principle applied to 5/8 and 9/8.

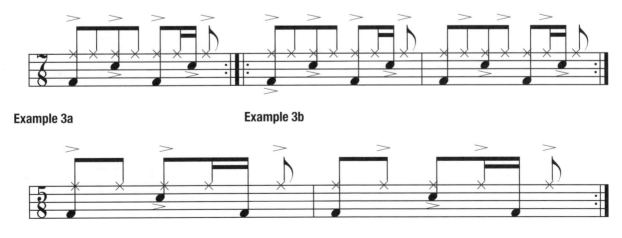

Example 3a   **Example 3b**

Example 4a

Example 4b

Examples 5–7 below show more examples of 5/8, 7/8 and 9/8 grooves. Try playing them in the same way, using this two-measure right-hand pattern. I've avoided writing the right hand for these examples to allow them to be practised with other ostinatos. For example, Examples 8a–8c show Examples 5c, 6d and 7c played with some different right-hand ostinatos.

As I mentioned earlier, the best way of getting fluent with the various different feels is to play them. Try getting together with some other musicians and jamming these time signatures and, who knows, maybe even taking a solo in them!

Example 5a   **Example 5b**   **Example 5c**

Example 5d   **Example 5e**   **Example 5f**

Example 6a   **Example 6b**

Example 6c   **Example 6d**

Example 6e   **Example 6f**

Example 7a   **Example 7b**

Example 7c   **Example 7d**

Example 7e   **Example 7f**

Example 8a

Example 8b

Example 8c

Latin

The last few years have seen much interest in Afro-Cuban and Brazilian rhythms applied to the drums, with players such as Horacio 'El Negro' Hernandez scaling new heights of co-ordination and musicality. In this section, I'm going to take a look some of the basic Latin (including Brazilian) rhythms in use today. Even if you've no intention of playing any Latin music at any point, I'm sure you'll still benefit from the musicality and coordination to be derived from these time feels.

Bossa Nova

The bossa nova is a Brazilian rhythm which you've probably heard played along with tunes such as 'The Girl From Ipanema'. It's built around the cross-stick part, played in the left hand and usually over a slow samba bass-drum pattern, although playing 1 and 3 on the bass drum will also work. The right hand, which can be played on the hi-hats or ride, can be played flat without accents or it can follow the cross pattern. In quieter situations, you can play the cross-stick part as accents within eighth notes on the hi-hat (Example 1).

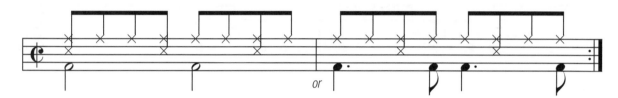

Example 1

Samba

This style (Example 2a) is usually based around the following bass-drum/hi-hat ostinato. Beat 3 is often accentuated on the surdo drum, which you can imitate by moving between the ride cymbal and floor tom (Example 2b, while Examples 2c and 2d also incorporate

the low tom for this effect). In all of these exercises, the left hand stays on the snare, apart from Example 2c, where it moves between the snare and hi-hat.

As an extra challenge to develop more fluidity, try soloing over the foot ostinato with the hands (check out the ostinato solos in the next chapter).

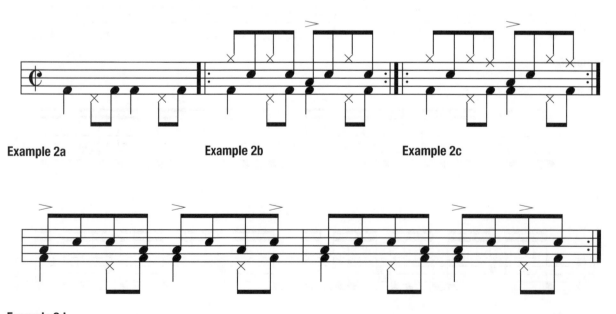

Example 2a   **Example 2b**   **Example 2c**

Example 2d

Another approach to playing a samba is based around playing an ostinato in the right hand as well as the bass drum. The ostinato is intended to imitate the triangle pattern often heard in a samba. In this case we're going to play an eighth/two-16th-note pattern. Example 3 shows some different ways of developing this, as well as some left-hand independence. A nice-sounding left-hand pattern is shown in Example 4, starting on measure 1 or measure 2, almost like the clave played forward and reverse (more on that soon). One of these variations will work well in most situations.

The next step for developing independence with the left hand would be to work through Reading Texts A and B (pages 47–8) with the left hand while maintaining the ostinato in the right. Example 5 shows the first four measures of Reading Text B played in this way.

Example 3

Example 4

Example 5

Afro-Cuban Grooves

Next we'll move up to Cuba for some Afro-Cuban patterns. It's important to remember that the drum set has no part in traditional Afro-Cuban music, so the aim is to imitate the various sounds heard in the percussion section. Most Afro-Cuban music is based around a rhythmic pulse called the *clave* (pronounced *clah-vay*), which is Spanish for 'key'. Understanding the clave is essential for playing Afro-Cuban music. Let's begin by looking at the two different clave patterns. The son clave is the older, original clave, different from the more syncopated rumba clave, but by only one note. Both of these patterns can be played forward or reverse, 3/2 or 2/3, the 3s and 2s referring to the number of notes in each measure. This might seem complicated, as we now have four patterns, but there isn't too much to remember and you'll find that only one of them sits within the tune you're playing (Example 6).

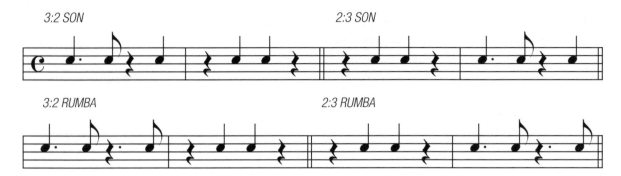

Example 6

Now let's look at the pattern normally played by the timbale player. The right-hand part, the *cascara* (meaning 'shell'), gets its name from the fact that it's normally played on the shell of timbales while the left hand plays the clave as a cross-stick. We can imitate the sound of the timbale shell by playing the pattern on the shell of the floor tom, but it can also be played on a cowbell, the ride cymbal, hi-hats or even the rims. I've written this here (Example 7) with both the son and rumba clave, but only in 3/2, so be sure to practise it reversed.

We can now add the bass drum. Examples 8a–8c show three of the most commonly used bass drum patterns in Afro-Cuban music. The first is playing the *bombo* note. This is the note emphasised by the

conguero, or conga player's patterns, and is normally played on only the second note of the clave.

The second pattern is the *tumbao*. This figure is often played by the bass player in Afro-Cuban music. Here the emphasis should fall on the 'and' of 2.

The same applies to the third pattern the *baiao* (pronounced 'buy-own'). To develop these last two patterns try soloing over them with the hands; you could begin with single strokes, moving on to paradiddles and so on. You could also try imitating the whole of the conga part by moving the left hand between the cross-stick on the snare and the toms.

Examples 9a–9c demonstrate three different variations on the rhythms in Examples 8a–8c, each shown with one of the three bass-drum variations.

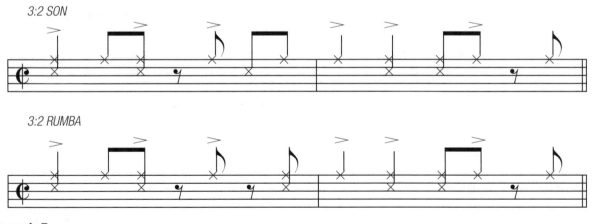

Example 7

Example 8a

Example 8b

Example 8c

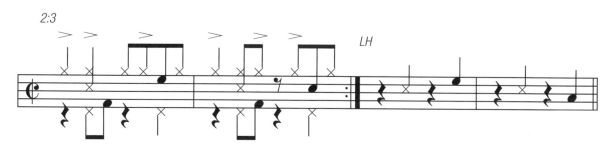

Example 9a

Example 9b

Example 9c

The above examples will work well in most salsa situations, but we can apply the same variations to the mambo bell pattern, which can again be played forward or reverse, but usually with the son clave.

Examples 10a and 10b show it played with the clave pattern in the left hand. Notice the placement of the accents, which although tricky to achieve is an integral part of the feel.

2:3

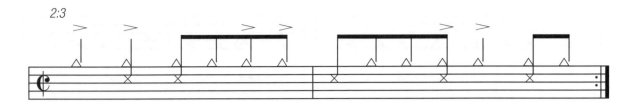

Example 10a

3:2

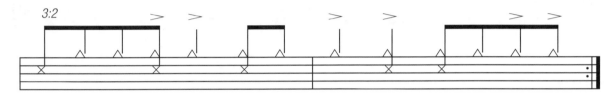

Example 10b

Mozambique

Another popular Afro-Cuban pattern is the *mozambique*, which is ironically just a name and has nothing to do with the African nation. This pattern applies particularly well to the drum set and has been demonstrated wonderfully by Steve Gadd on many occasions.

Again there's a bell pattern to learn, which, although similar to the *cascara*, is more syncopated. Examples 11 shows some variations, concluding with the version played often by Steve Gadd. Notice how, regardless of what happens to the bass drum or left hand, the right-hand pattern remains constant throughout.

Example 11

Songo

Next up is an Afro-Cuban style that actually started life being played on the drum set. The style is called *songo*, and Changuito (drummer for the Cuban band Los Van Van) is credited as coming up with the basic pattern,

which is actually quite simple in comparison to some of the previous examples, inasmuch as the right hand plays just 1 and 3 most of the time.

Example 12 shows some variations on the basic feel of songo.

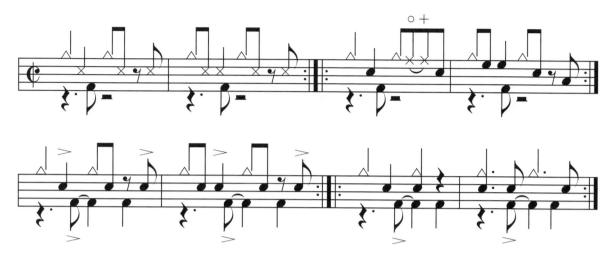

Example 12

Afro-Cuban 6/8

Our final Latin groove is the Afro-Cuban 6/8 – or, as it's sometimes referred to, the *bembe*. Again, there is a clave running through it that is very similar to the rumba clave, and again, throughout all of the variations the right hand remains unaffected.

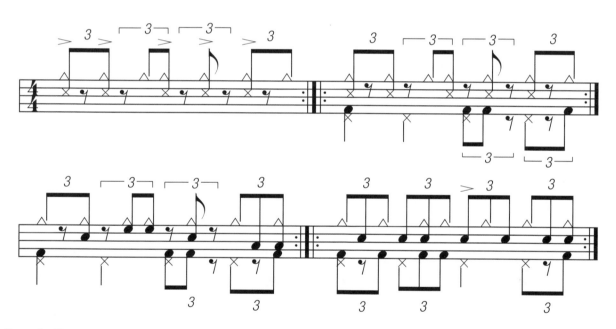

Example 13

As I said earlier, even if you have no intention of playing any Latin music, these patterns will provide very musical additions to your playing, not to mention develop your co-ordination. If this has whetted your appetite, two of the best books I've seen dedicated to this subject are *Latin Grooves* by Dave Hassell and *Afro-Cuban Rhythms For The Drum Set* by Frank Malabe and Bob Weiner.

5 DRUM SET VOCABULARY

If I had a pound for every time I've been asked by a student to show them some fills, I'd be writing this from a beach house in the Bahamas. But seriously, it seems that a lot of drummers want a shortcut to developing a vocabulary on the kit, and I think the danger here can be simply showing or learning licks that have no direct relevance to any music. One of the most important things is in drumming is to have the ability to incorporate fill ideas within your playing, and this is as dependent on phrasing ideas such as the double- and six-stroke-roll concepts seen earlier as the fill itself. In other words, getting into and out of the fill is as important as the fill itself. Hopefully, if you've worked through some of the other exercises in this book, you'll be halfway to developing a good foundation in time playing and rudiments. Combined with some of the ideas shown here, you should be able to incorporate them fluidly.

I've tried to avoid writing out specific fills so that, once the basic exercises can be played, you can begin to apply them in ways that sound good to you.

The Feet…

Let's begin with what can be a much-neglected area: the feet. With all the focus on rudiments and hands, sometimes I think it's important to isolate the feet just to check that everything's in order. The following exercises are based around a quarter-note pulse played with the left foot on the hi-hat and a variety of figures played with the bass drum. These exercises are great for ironing out any co-ordination discrepancies between the feet. The first exercise (Example 1) simply jumps a subdivision in each measure, so be sure to start out at a tempo at which you can play 16th notes on the bass drum.

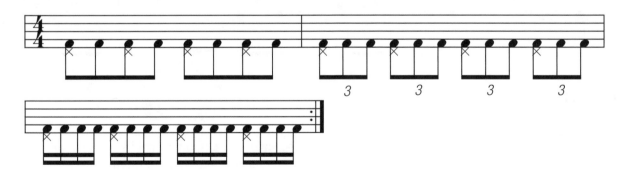

Example 1

Examples 2a–2e use different groupings on the bass drum, played over two measures.

90

Example 2a

Example 2b

Example 2c

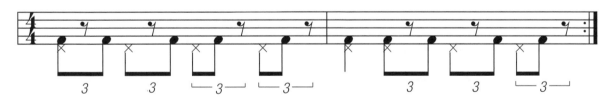

Example 2d

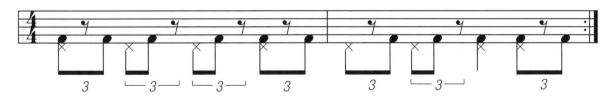

Example 2e

Examples 3a–3e use the same figures but with a pick-up note added, making co-ordination more demanding.

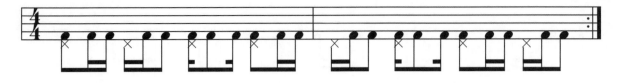

Example 3a

Example 3b

Example 3c

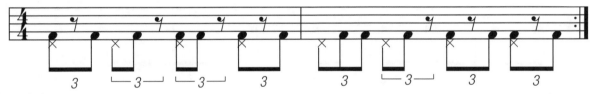

Example 3d

Example 3e

...And The Hands

Now let's look at some exercises incorporating the hands. What follows are some simple hand/foot combinations in both 16th-note and eighth-note triplet feels (Examples 4a, 4b). Once you're able to play the basic figures, try adding the left foot on quarter notes. This can be tricky, so be patient – it's well worth the effort. Whenever I've worked on this kind of material, I've always practised it with the hi-hat playing time, whether that be quarter notes, eighth notes or 2 and

4 (in the more up-tempo jazz applications). By developing this, the left foot helps to maintain the pulse, enabling the listener and band members to hear the time, even though it's no longer being played. If you need any more convincing, check out the wonderful soloing of Steve Gadd, Dave Weckl or Vinnie Colaiuta. I've purposely avoided writing out all of the possible permutations, sticking instead with those that sound good and are easy to apply. Be sure to try moving your hands around different parts of the kit.

Example 4a

Example 4b

Doubles Strokes Around The Kit

One of the best ways to develop strength within the double stroke is to move it around the kit, especially to the toms. Obviously the larger, lower-tuned drums are much harder to play doubles on so really require some effort to get the sticks moving. But it also makes for some really slick-sounding fills, the sort of which you simply couldn't play using single strokes. All of the following exercises are written in 16th notes to make reading easier, but they're intended to be played as 32nd notes, hence the hi-hat notated on 1 and 3.

Example 5a shows a figure similar to that seen in the previous 16th-note exercises, but now it's played differently. This should be played first in the right hand, then the left, then alternating. It's a great warm-up for the remaining exercises, especially when practised moving around the kit.

The remaining figures – Examples 5b–5g – will all make great fill ideas. Try practising them by playing three bars of time then one repeat of the exercise.

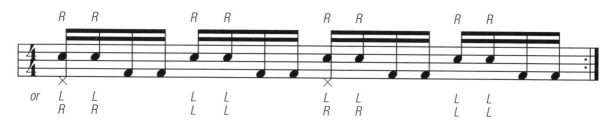

Example 5a

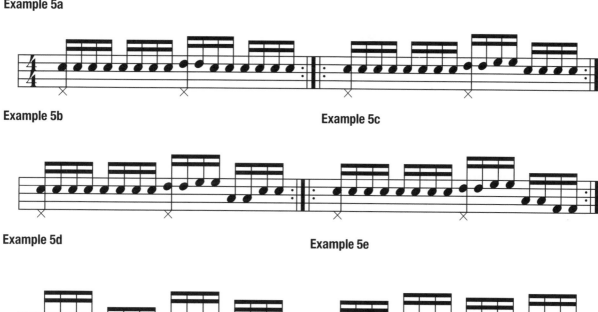

Example 5b   **Example 5c**

Example 5d   **Example 5e**

Example 5f   **Example 5g**

Double Stops

As drummers, most of our time is spent developing the ability to play four different things at once, so here's a concept that involves both right and left hand playing the same thing together. It's something that most drummers have toyed with at some point, but here, instead of a few fills, you'll find a way of phrasing using this concept.

Example 6a illustrates a two-measure phrase based around groups of three: snare, kick, snare. This exercise – and all of these eighth-note phrases for that matter – can be practised in two ways: firstly, with the hi-hat on 2 and 4, they can be played in a jazz or swing context; secondly, if played with the hi-hat on 1 and 3, they can be played as one bar of 16th notes.

Example 6a

Example 6b uses a similar idea but this time using a group of five: snare, kick, snare, kick, snare. With all of the following exercises, the figures notated on the snare are to be played with both hands simultaneously. This can be done by playing the right hand on a tom and the left on the snare (Example 7a), or the same thing but with the left hand on the hi-hat (Example 7b). This creates a nice-sounding open-hi-hat effect if both of your feet take care of playing the bass-drum part.

Example 6b

Example 7a   **Example 7b**

The next step is playing two notes with the bass drum. Examples 8a and 8b show the same basic figures as were used in Example 1 but this time substituting the last snare of each grouping with a bass drum. This concept will also work well in a triplet rate. Be sure to try playing the left foot on quarter notes (Examples 9a–9f); it might be hard at first, but keep persevering.

Example 8a

Example 8b

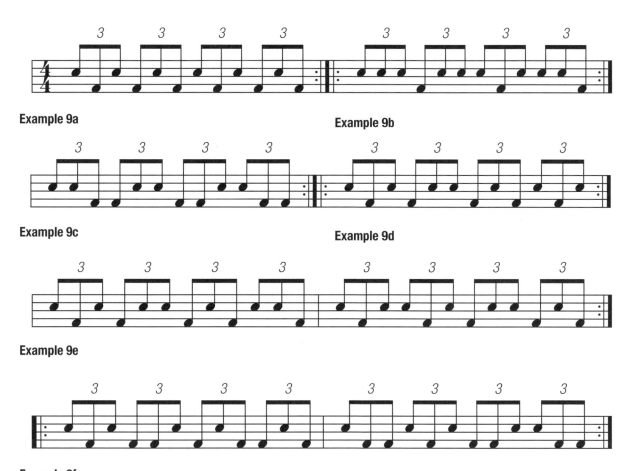

Example 9a

Example 9b

Example 9c

Example 9d

Example 9e

Example 9f

These last examples use a great variation of the figures looked at so far that involves playing both left and right cymbals together on the second of all groups of two played on the bass drum. Examples 10a and 10b show how to develop the basic idea, with 10c and 10d showing it applies to examples 9a and 9d. Meanwhile, Examples 11a and 11b show this idea applied to Examples 8b and 9f.

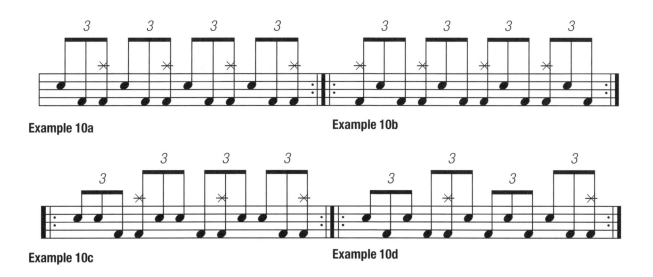

Example 10a

Example 10b

Example 10c

Example 10d

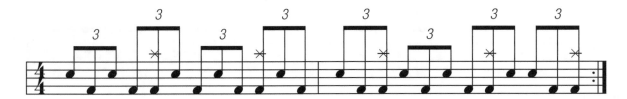

Example 11a

Example 11b

This is a fill-and-soloing idea that was used extensively by Tony Williams and can also be heard in the playing of Vinnie Colaiuta and Steve Smith (both big Tony Williams fans, incidentally). When Vinnie uses these kinds of phrases, he often flams the figures between the toms, which can sound really powerful, and Steve Smith is a master at moving these ideas around the kit. Either way, they make a great addition to any drummer's arsenal.

Ostinato Soloing

'It has always seemed to me that a concise, well-paced solo always elicits positive audience response. Can this really be self-indulgent?'
Neil Peart

The drum solo can be the best part of the gig for some people (usually drummers) or the part where everyone goes to the bar (often the rest of the audience).

There are a couple of different types of solo situations. For example, there's the four-bar break in a song, the classic 'give the drummer some' solo. Then there's soloing over a vamp, where the band plays a repeated figure as a backdrop to the solo. Similar to this is soloing over 'hits' or accents played by the band every so often. All of these examples have one thing in common: they're not really solos *per se*. Far more daunting is the open solo, where the rest of

the band – and, if it's not going particularly well, the audience – go to the bar. In any of these situations, it's very easy to fall into the trap of 'now I'll show you what I can do', and before you know it you're playing as fast and as loud as you can and… Well, I want to go to the bar just thinking about it.

A drum solo is our opportunity to show our drumming prowess, but prowess isn't just made up of fast licks; it's our musicality, our sense of dynamics, pace, form, tension and so on. In that respect, it's a good idea to think about where you want the solo to go. Do you want to start the solo with a huge impact, dropping it down in the middle and building it up for the climax? Or do you want to build it up gradually, increasing the intensity before dropping back down, drawing the listener in with you? Perhaps if the solo's within a tune, you want to keep a groove going, soloing within it.

If, however, you have an open solo, having some component parts to work from can help. For example, you could think of it as a song form, starting with the initial pattern – let's call it A. At this point, the audience are tapping their feet. Then, after a bit of messing around with that theme and perhaps a tempo change or change of dynamics, we go to section B (the audience nods in approval at the subtle change of pace). Then, after building it up, we hit section C, the cool Simon Phillips-esque polyrhythm, and the audience is clapping (some in seven, some in four).

Then, with a bit of musical sleight of hand, you're back into the intro groove, A, and the audience is on its feet.

Or how about this scenario: you begin your solo with a really fast funk groove – at this point the audience is trying to tap along. You then add the really cool double-pedal thing you can almost play up to speed. People exchange glances. Time to get into the really intense 'tribally' thing you worked on – but only at a much slower tempo. The audience is getting restless (and thirsty). You finally grab the reins to get it under control, to take a run at the final fence: the Virgil Donati lick. Well, at least it sounded something like the way you practised

it! You stand up to bask in the warmth of the rapturous applause to discover the audience going…well, to the bar. OK, an exaggeration maybe, but I know which gig I would have preferred to have been at.

One way of giving an open solo some context is to introduce an ostinato with the feet and solo over it. Below (Examples 7a–7e) are some different ostinatos which not only make fun solo themes but also make great warm-up and co-ordination exercises. In Examples 7a, 7b and 7c, the left foot can also be played on the auxiliary bass drum pedal or, if spread across the two, on both the hi-hat and the auxiliary pedals.

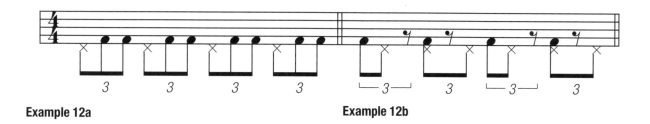

Example 12a

Example 12b

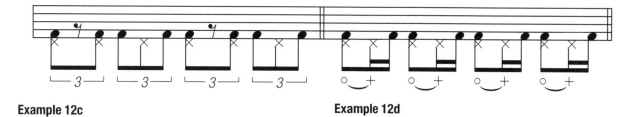

Example 12c

Example 12d

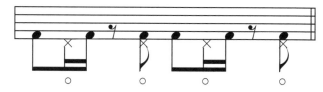

Example 12e

Whatever you choose to play in your solo, remember that, just as with songs, people like to hear hooks or motifs, whether that's a specific rhythm you continually refer to or a melodic idea around the toms.

Space is also a useful tool and can help a solo to breathe. Try listening to the melodic soloing of Max Roach and Terry Bozzio for some inspiration in creating a musical solo.

6 READING

'I've met too many readers who are crap players. I'd sooner work with a non-reader I can speak to, but that player is no good if you've got 50 minutes to learn, say, 16 numbers.' Dave Hassell

If you've bought this book yet are unable to read notation, firstly I don't think it will be a problem as I've presented everything in such a way that, along with the accompanying CD, all of the examples should be easy enough to understand, if not play! I do however think that you're missing out on an important aspect of music. Being able to play through a piece of music that you've never heard in your life and have it sound like you know it is a wonderful, not to mention useful thing. There are those who argue that reading isn't very 'rock 'n' roll', yet on my first gig with Republica in front of a festival crowd of 30,000 people I had to read charts simply because I hadn't enough time to learn the set. With the charts written on discreet cheat sheets, which had just enough info on them such as basic grooves and chorus – 'eight bars, verse ten', etc – I made it through the show.

There's also the fact that you're able to transcribe and analyse your favourite drummers' playing, which is a very useful practice tool. Talking of which, if you can read, you can then write out your own ideas.

'Reading is an aid to memory. That's all it is. You get 100 yards down the road after a lesson, and if there's nothing written down, I guarantee they'll have forgotten.' Dave Hassell

For those of you for whom reading drum notation is a relatively new experience, here I'd like to explain the basic principles. In simple terms, it's just maths, and fortunately for us, easy maths at that. To begin with, Example 1 shows all of the different note values and their respective rests. The notes are used to show us where there is sound and the rests indicate silence.

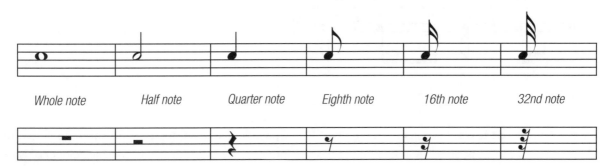

Whole note   Half note   Quarter note   Eighth note   16th note   32nd note

Example 1

Most contemporary musicians use the American terminology (above the stave), whereas the English names are still used by the majority of classical musicians (below the stave). When more than one of the notes has value of less than one beat and are placed next to each other, they're *beamed* together (although not across the middle of the bar) in order to make it somewhat easier to read, as shown in Example 2.

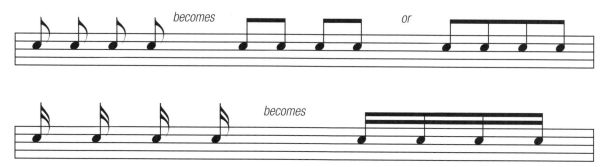

Example 2

To equate these notes and values with familiar sounds, when we count off a tune we're counting quarter notes. If we fill in the spaces between these notes, we get eighth notes, then 16ths and 32nd notes and so on. There are also subdivisions in between these. For example, if we evenly fit three notes where we previously had two, we have a triplet, as illustrated in Example 3.

Quarter-note triplets   Eighth-note triplets

Sixteenth-note triplets

Example 3

Our basic subdivisions of eighth note, eighth-note triplet and 16th notes can all be counted phonetically in order to get a feel for the subdivision. Eighth notes can be counted as 1 +, 2 +, 3 +, 4 + and so on (the + being 'and'); eighth-note triplets can be counted as 1 trip-let, 2 trip-let, 3 trip-let, 4 trip-let; while 16th notes can be counted as 1 e + a, 2 e + a, 3 e + a, 4 e + a.

Unfortunately, not everything you'll ever play is made up of the same subdivision with a variety of combinations used. This is where the maths comes in. Take a look at Example 4, which uses a combination of eighth and 16th notes. Notice how they're beamed in such a way that it's clear where each new beat falls, with each group adding up to four 16ths.

1 (e) + a 2 (c) + a 3 e + (a) 4 e + a

Example 4

OK. But what happens if we want an eighth note to fall somewhere other than on an eighth note – in other words, on an upbeat 16th? This will throw the whole measure out of sync, as you'd no longer be able to see where each beat falls. The solution comes in the form of a tie (Example 5). This can be placed between notes and adds the value of the second note onto to the first yet still allows you to see individual beats and bar lines.

1   (a)   +   a   (2)   e   +   (a)   3   e   (+)   a   (4)   (e)   +   (a)

Example 5

How about if we want a note to last for somewhere in between an eighth note and a quarter note – say, for three 16th notes? Of course, we could tie an eighth note to a 16th note. However, an easier solution is to 'dot' an eighth note, as shown in Example 6. Dotting a note adds half its value again.

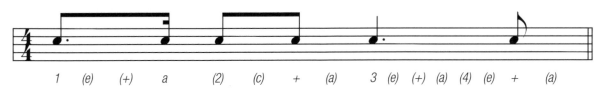

1   (e)   (+)   a   (2)   (c)   +   (a)   3   (e)   (+)   (a)   (4)   (e)   +   (a)

Example 6

In Example 6, beat 1 is worth three 16th notes, so the next note is on the 'a' of 1. This is the equivalent of a 16th note tied to an eighth note, making it worth three 16th notes, so the next note will fall on the '+' of 2. On beat 3 is a dotted quarter note (which means it's now worth a beat and a half), meaning that the next note falls on the 'and' of 4.

Dots and ties can often seem irrelevant to drummers, as most of the sounds we play are short, but it's important to remember that melodic instruments are able to hold notes. For this reason, it's important to appreciate how long a note is sounded for. For example, if when reading a chart we see a 16th note and a dotted eighth note together it would make sense to play a short sound followed by a long one, perhaps a snare followed by a bass drum and cymbal. This is especially important when playing figures with the rest of the band, a skill most big-band drummers have down to a fine art.

'I'm sure even the best drummers get lost within charts. It's just that they're better at covering it up.' *Billy Ward*

As well as note values, each instrument on the kit is allocated its own space or symbol. Funnily enough, this is actually a grey area, with different books and charts using different lines, spaces and even symbols, although in the last few years there's been a concerted effort to use a universal notation. Throughout this book, I've used this notation, as shown in Example 7.

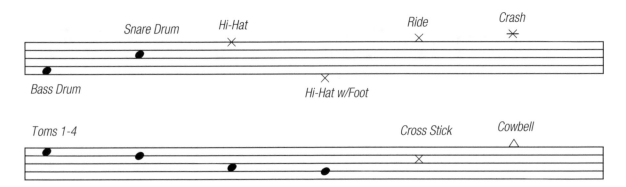

Example 7

When dealing with drums, most patterns can be written one of two ways, depending on the nature of the pattern. For example, a pattern with an ostinato in the hands is much easier to read if the hands are separated from the feet, with the hands written from the top of the stave and the feet the bottom. In Example 8a, we need to separate the various parts as well as negotiate the subdivisions, whereas in Example 8b we can simply glance at what the hands are doing and read the bass drum part as we would a piece of reading text.

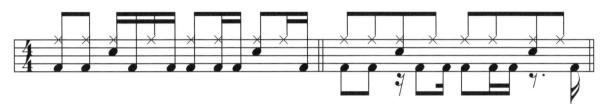

Example 8a   **Example 8b**

Another situation would be if there is no constant such as a fill or linear-type pattern, where separating the bass drum makes reading difficult (Example 9). I'm sure that, like me, you find Example 9b easier to read.

Example 9a   **Example 9b**

It's also important to differentiate between different types of reading. For example, being able to read snare-drum solos doesn't make you a good chart reader. They're very different animals, with a chart often containing very little 'drum' information, such as grooves. Instead it will convey the form, dynamics and feel of a tune and can sometimes even come in the form of a chord chart, with no drum part whatsoever. Even a well-written drum chart can leave a lot to the drummer's interpretation, and it's often been said that the most useful thing required when sight-reading is a good set of ears!

As you can see, in its simplest terms reading really is basic maths, but obviously an experienced reader isn't adding up note values as they read a piece of music; instead they've developed the ability to recognise figures instinctively in the same way as you would read a book. To reach this level requires practice, just like the rest of your drumming. You could begin by playing through some reading text on the snare drum. On the CD, I've included versions of me playing the four reading texts shown earlier for just this purpose. There are also other books you could try the same thing with, such as Louis Belson's *Modern Reading Text in 4/4* or Gary Chester's *New Breed* (a great book, by the way!).

Another way to develop reading skills is transcribing. You could begin with something simple such as a basic groove eventually working up to entire transcriptions. Writing out your own charts is also good practice.

There will always be incredible players who are non-readers and have never found it a problem, such as Buddy Rich and Dennis Chambers, but for the rest of us mortals being able to read can make a huge difference to our drumming. And don't be put off by those who claim it's not very rock 'n' roll – they're usually the ones who can't read!

7 DRUM SOUNDS

Drum sounds can be very subjective – after all, we all have our own interpretations of what sounds 'good'. There are also lots of factors involved – shells, bearing edges, heads, tuning and suspension – and these are just when dealing with acoustic situations. In the studio or on stage, there are the mics, their placement, EQing and processing to consider, among other things. So, where do we begin? Well, let's start with the room in which the drums are being played.

Acoustic Environment

Have you ever tried out a drum or cymbal in a drum shop, got it home and found it sounded very different? In an acoustic environment, we're relying solely on the sound of the kit for projection, but there are also other factors that will colour the sound of the kit, namely reflections. What you hear when a drum kit is played in a room is not just the kit itself but rather the initial sound followed almost immediately by its reflected sound from various surfaces within the room. These reflections can have a massive effect upon how the kit appears to sound. For example, if you were to play a kit in a small carpeted room, with heavy curtains, the reflections would be fairly minimal, with the kit appearing to sound small. If you then took the same kit and played it in a large wooden-floored hall, it would sound much bigger, with more reflections that take longer to reach your ears, thus giving the impression of a 'bigger' sound.

The extreme opposite of this would be playing the same kit in a field, where there are no reflective surfaces. The same kit would sound flat and dead. Kits often sound this way on big stages, especially festival stages, where, with no reflective surfaces, the drums can have a dry, lifeless sound. It's worth considering this when taking your new purchase from the large showroom to your smaller drum room. You could try taking along other drums or cymbals to serve as comparison.

In a live acoustic situation, another important aspect to consider is the fact that your kit will sound lower in pitch the further away from it you are (think about the way a police siren becomes lower in pitch as it drives past you). This is important because those low booming toms that sound great from behind the kit can sound like the cases they arrived in from 20 feet away.

'I tune my drums higher for more projection'
Simon Phillips

And what about dynamics? 'Dynamics? Whaddaya mean dynamics? I'm hittin' 'em as hard as I can!' If you're the only acoustic instrument on the stage, which is often the case in rehearsal or small gig situations, your volume should dictate the overall volume of the band. With this in mind, it's important to keep your volume consistent (or at least in keeping with the material being played). It can be easy to get carried away and start overplaying, playing the cymbals louder and forcing the band to turn up. This usually means it's harder to hear the bass drum, so you in turn play harder and a vicious circle is created.

Sound Reinforcement

Most larger gigs require mics to be placed at various points around the kit, and what actually gets miked usually depends on the size of the PA and venue or the number of mics used. The first instrument to get a mic is usually the bass drum because lower frequencies require more power (take a look at the wattage of your bass player's rig versus your guitarist's). Next up would be the toms and snare, and finally the overheads and hi-hat (unless it is a jazz or acoustic-style gig, in which case just a bass drum and overheads might be used).

As soon as close mics on individual drums are used the choice of tuning become a factor. For example, if you've been used to playing in an acoustic situation and tuned the toms higher for extra cut (and maybe removed some dampening from the bass drum for a little extra 'boom'), you may well find the toms too lively or 'ringy' and the kick too long once amplified through a PA. And if, when asked to do something about the sound, you're either reluctant to change it, you don't want to use tape on your new heads or you're just plain unable to lose the ring, the engineer needs to gate the tail end of the sound out to obtain a 'clean' mix at volume. This is fine in professional situations, where gating is the norm, but smaller gigs may not have the relevant outboard gear. Drums ringing for several seconds in the studio might sound natural, but when dealing with drums through large PAs the drums themselves begin to resonate in response to their own amplified sound, which in turn is picked up by the mics, causing feedback hell! Unfortunately, to solve this problem, some engineers over-gate, especially if they're not aware of how the drummer plays dynamically, so make sure during the soundcheck that everything you're playing is making it into the PA. In other words, play the quietest you're going to play, and if you're unable to hear it in the room then ask the FOH (front-of-house) engineer to loosen the threshold on the relevant drum (usually the bass drum, but sometimes the snare).

Drum Suspension

So that's enough about the room. What about the drums themselves? These days modern production techniques pretty much guarantee that most drums shells are going to be perfectly round, although years ago that wasn't the case. Another aspect that's improved is the cutting of the bearing edges, which is far more accurate than ever. As a result, today's drums are easier to tune, hold their tuning better and have more attack. However,

some people prefer the mellow sound of vintage drums, though I can't help feeling that, when it comes to vintage gear, we're often guilty of listening with our eyes.

Another aspect of drum construction to change over the last few years is how the drum is mounted to the hardware. Years ago, all manufacturers mounted their drums directly onto the hardware, with the tom arm either clamping vertically through a tom clamp or actually through the clamp and into the shell itself. If you have a drum kit where the toms mount this way, try lifting off a rack tom and hitting it whilst holding it by the rim. The drum, if tuned well, should sound full and resonant. Now place the drum back onto its clamp and you should notice a marked reduction in resonance and bottom-end presence. It's because of this restriction of resonance that Gary Gauger first created the RIMS (Resonance Isolation Mounting System) nearly 20 years ago. This, along with double pedals and plastic drum heads, could be regarded as one of the most important inventions after the drum set itself. Now, most manufacturers have their equivalent of the RIMS mount, all of which are designed to enable the toms to resonate freely. This resonance increases bottom end, which in turn allows a more open tuning to be used and hence achieves a bigger tom sound. Some companies have also looked into mounting snare drums and bass drums this way, but because of their comparatively short sounds it's much harder to perceive their effect.

If you don't have a isolation mounts, try mounting toms at the ends of the arms for a more open sound and avoid over-tightening the snare basket as this can not only choke the drum but distort the bottom hoop.

Drum Head Choice

'I do prefer thinner heads, for the reason that I can play quietly and still get the tone from the drums. When I think of a drum set with thick heads, I feel I'm going to have to hit them hard to get them to speak.' *Jim Keltner*

Is your playing situation loud or quiet? Do you need good stick response with bright overtones or the reverse with a controlled tone? Let's take a look at the different head types available.

- **Single Ply-Clear (Light)** – These heads are generally used as bottom resonant heads, although they could be used for very light playing situations. They offer very fast response with lots of overtones and are suited to higher tunings.

- **Single Ply-Clear/Coated (Medium)** – This type of head has become the head of choice over the last few years. They're usually used as top heads, although they can be used as more controlled bottom heads. They offer a good balance of tone versus overtone, are suited to medium to high tunings and can be used in most musical situations.

- **Double Ply-Clear/Coated (Medium)** – One step towards a more controlled sound and suited to slightly louder playing situations, this double-ply head comprises two lightweight heads with a thin layer of oil trapped between them. These heads are happier in a mid-to-low tuning and offer slightly more subdued stick response. This is even more apparent with the coated version.

- **Double Ply-Clear/Coated (Heavy)** – Years ago, when drum sounds were much drier, the drum heads of choice were usually Remo Pinstripes and Evans Hydraulics. These consisted of two medium-weight heads separated by a layer of oil. These heads are suited to low tunings and have few overtones.

- **Tone Controlled Heads** – There are various heads available that offer some form of dampening built in. These can come in the form of a gasket around the outside of the head or a patch stuck on the underside of the head at the centre. They both help to reduce high overtones and create a more focused sound. The heads with a centre dot are often used on snare drums to reinforce the head, while the gasket version is often used on bass drums to help reduce high-end overtones.

With these choices at your disposal, it should help you find the right head for any given situation. For example,

on a quiet jazz or acoustic gig, heavy double-ply heads could sound choked and dull, while a thin single-ply head will firstly struggle to withstand the poundings of a rock gig but might also lack the fundamental tone needed to cut through a mix.

Tuning

The way in which a drum is tuned can have a massive impact on its sound. A top-of-the-range maple-shelled custom drum can be made to sound like a budget drum if poorly tuned, and vice versa. Some years ago one drum company claimed that the drum heads create 80 per cent of the drum's sound, and if you've ever heard any of the 'shell-free' kits that are available, you can start to believe it.

We've looked at different drum-head types, so let's consider tension and tuning. Tuning a new head requires seating it onto the drum. This is best done by placing the head on the shell and tightening the lugs finger-tight and then, with your hand in the centre of the drum, pressing down and moving around the lugs, tightening one-quarter of a turn at a time. Once all of the wrinkles are out, tap at each lug using your finger and tune up the lowest lug each time. This process must be done with the opposite head muted, either on a carpet or your leg. If you try tuning a drum when it's on a stand, it becomes impossible to hear the individual heads.

Once the lugs are sounding similar, press heavily in the centre of the head to seat it again. At this point, you might hear the glue around the hoop crack. This is perfectly normal! Repeat the process until the drum begins to hold its tuning. At this point, you may find that the head is higher than you want it, so turn each lug down a quarter turn, press in the centre, and tune again.

Tune your drums for the situation. For example, if it's a quiet jazz gig, tune high. Without a high tuning there will be no tone or response at low volume, and vice versa. For a loud rock gig, while a high tuning could be used, the drums will lack depth and body and may sound better with a medium-to-low tuning.

Relative Tensions

You can usually hear when the drum is in its tuning range as it will sound full and boom, as opposed to producing a bang or boing if it's too high or a thud if too low (excuse the technical terminology!). The relative tension between the heads can also have a profound effect, especially on tom sounds. For example, if both heads are tuned to the same pitch – especially if it's the pitch of the shell – the drum will resonate for the longest possible time. Tuning the top head down from this will put the drum out of tune with itself, causing a pitch bend (this can also be achieved by detuning one of the top lugs one-quarter of a turn). It will also emphasise the stick's attack. Reversing this process and tuning the bottom head higher than the top will have a less positive effect on the drum's sound: the drum will sound choked and dead, with the added problem of increased overtones from the higher tensioned bottom head.

With the bass drum, a good rule of thumb is to go as low as possible before the head wrinkles – unless, of course, you're planning on playing some bebop, where the bass drum is tuned like another tom and is much higher than contemporary pop and rock tunings. For a deep, thunderous bass drum, the front head should also be tuned low. Listen for any high overtones, as this can dramatically affect how the depth of the drum is perceived.

Snare drums are very different animals and can be tuned anywhere from really high or really low, but it's generally a good idea to tune a drum to itself. In other words, if you have a seven-inch-deep wood drum it may well be suited to lower tunings, while a five-inch metal drum may sound better tuned high. If you do prefer the batter head tuned high, you could try keeping the snare head tuned slightly lower; this can add body and depth whilst maintaining the 'crack' of the top head. For most situations, however, tuning the bottom head just above the top will usually yield good results.

Dampening

'My drums project more than other drummers' because I tune them very differently. Most drummers tune lower than I do, and they put dampening on as well. That's going to take away from volume. My drums are very dynamic. They all have double heads, including the kick drums, so I get a lot of projection, especially from the bass drums.' *Simon Phillips*

Choosing the right head should usually negate the need for dampening the head using tape and so on. For example, if you've been used to using a single-ply coated head but find the need to use tape to calm down some of the overtones, try moving up to a thin double-ply head. It's also worth remembering that the overtones that you may feel the need to eliminate in a studio situation will actually partly get lost in the mix and will also be what make your drum kit sound real. If the kit sounds boxy and lacking overtones before the other instruments are added, by the end of the mix, as everything competes for its place, the drums will be left sounding dull and lifeless.

Sticking tape on your drums is obviously a quick and easy solution to unwanted overtones, but there are other options. Years ago, drums would come supplied with internal dampeners made of felt which would press onto the underside of the head. However, while convenient, these would often choke the drum. The new equivalent, developed by Dave Weckl, is mounted on the top head and actually lifts off the head when it's struck. This enables the drum's open tone to briefly ring through until the dampener drops back down to mute the unwanted aftertones. Other simpler ways of controlling overtones are moon gel (a silicon-like substance that can be easily removed) and zero rings, which work in the same way as the gasket fitted to the tone control heads, but again can be easily removed.

It's important to realise that these last methods really work only on batter heads; on toms it's often the bottom head that causes the drum to resonate longer than required. In these situations, a small amount of tape applied to the outer edge of the bottom head should help reduce unwanted overtones while retaining the depth and fullness of the drum.

Bass Drums

The bass drum is usually the one element of the kit that definitely needs some form of dampening. One exception to this might be an 18" drum tuned for a jazz gig, but even then under the scrutiny of a microphone there may well be unwanted high overtones. These highs detract from the low end of the drum, and the front head is usually where a few of these overtones tend to slip through. If, for example, you dampen the batter head but leave the front head, you might not hear the overtones but a mic will.

Some drummers use a completely open-tuned kick drum, which acoustically sounds huge, but in the studio it can be difficult to find a place in the mix for such a drum as it covers so many frequencies. The opposite of this is when a drummer stores his entire bedding inside the kick drum, resulting in it sounding like the box it came in. There are drummers and situations that require this type of sound: Dennis, Gadd and Vinnie often use this ultra-dead kick sound for a really tight, punchy sound. Simon Phillips, on the other hand, uses 24" bass drums with a rolled-up towel against the batter head and a smaller version on the front head. His front heads have no holes, with D-12 mics mounted inside, creating a massive, resonant sound. Steve Smith also uses relatively little dampening on his 20" drum, with just a felt strip on both heads. There's also another Dave Weckl-designed product based on Simon's rolled-up towel idea that clamps against the head, and there are other dampening pads available from Evans and DW.

As you can see, there are a lot of options out there, so while you can pay more than £1,000 for a top-of-the-range bass drum, simply throwing a pillow inside it probably won't be doing it justice.

Snare Buzz

A good rule of thumb for correcting snare tension is to tap with a stick in the centre of the head with the snares completely loose, then slowly tighten up the snares until they begin to sound crisp. That's all there is to it. Beware of over-tightening snares, though, as once they've been over-tightened they'll stretch – usually unevenly – and cause snare buzz. If you're still concerned with snare buzz, try turning off the snares while soundchecking the rest of the kit; when you begin to play the kit as a whole, the snare buzz will usually just blend in.

Some drummers try to reduce snare buzz by loosening the lugs next to the snares on the snare head. However, you should find that any excess snare buzz will usually get lost in the mix and may even add to the 'life' of the kit. If, however, you find one of the

toms really sets the snare buzzing excessively, the only solution is to adjust the tuning on either drum or try tuning one drum up and one down an eighth of a turn on each lug.

Mixing Your Acoustic Sound

'There are separate components, but they all make one instrument. Each component has to work in conjunction, sympathetically. Take away a few of those ringy toms or the second bass drum and in a way it's like taking away keys from a piano. They all make up part of the sound.'
Simon Phillips

If ten different drummers get up and play the same tune on the same kit, they'll all have a slightly different sound, approach and feel. One of the contributing factors in these differences can be the internal dynamics of the kit, and one of the most common problems in contemporary pop and rock situations is that of the bass drum being played too quietly. I've seen this a lot in drummers who perhaps practise on electronic kits or who have yet to develop heel-up technique. This light bass drum causes the drumming to lack weight.

Another problem can be that of the hi-hats being too loud. This can be especially problematic in the studio, where an over-enthusiastic drummer can have the hi-hats bleeding into the other mics, creating a real problem come mixdown. (This was, in fact, the reason why cymbal manufacturers started to create smaller hi-hats.)

Cymbals can create a similar problem if overplayed and will mean that the overhead mics are good only for picking up the cymbals when, in fact, they could be used to capture the bigger picture of the whole kit.

Another idea that can work well is that of playing the toms slightly harder than the rest of the kit. This can help the tom fills jump out and prevent them being overpowered by the snare drum. Also be aware when playing jazz time that nothing should really overpower the ride cymbal, unless intended. In jazz, unlike music with a backbeat, the time is stated by the right hand on the cymbal, as opposed to the bass drum and snare.

Another problem here can be if the bass drum is played or 'feathered' on quarter notes too loudly.

Feathering the bass drum is real art and, if done correctly, can really help to make time feel grounded. Check out some of the masters.

Internal dynamics are also important. If there's very little difference between the level of ghost notes and backbeats, the playing can seem one-dimensional. Try to get the ghost notes as quiet as possible while hitting a consistent rimshot backbeat. The same goes for the hi-hats, where you can move between the edge and the top of the cymbal, moving between the bell and bow.

Even the bass drum can be played with dynamics. Take a samba pattern, for instance. Here the emphasis will fall on the downbeats and, hey presto, dynamics! This same bass-drum technique should be applied to the rest of your playing.

You could also try viewing your playing as though you're behind a mixing desk. Have a quick look at the diagram below.

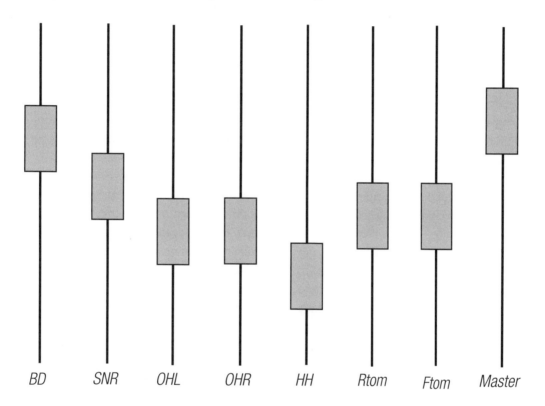

Selecting Drums

Again, choosing drums is a subjective thing. There are always going to be factors to sway you, aside from the obvious issue of how the drums sound. For instance, who endorses the drums you like? Do they make the colours/finishes you like? Do you like the hardware they require? And then we get to the more important stuff: do they make the sizes you want? What woods do they use and what sort of bearing edges do they have?

There are a lot of factors to consider, but let's begin with some simple points: what style and volume of music are you going to be playing? This will enable you to decide the sizes you require. For example, a kit with an 18" bass drum with 12" and 14" toms isn't really going to cut it with a loud metal band, and vice versa – that 24" kick probably isn't going to work in a quiet acoustic setting.

While on the subject of bass drums, these days a lot of drummers seem to be moving towards 20" bass drums. This size offers a lot of versatility and will cope with most situations but it will never move the air in the way a 22" drum can. As you can imagine, it's simply a case of assessing just what the drums are going to be used for. A good all-round kit these days seems to be the 20" bass drum combined with what are now, for some reason, called fusion sizes: 10", 12" and 14" toms. These tom sizes make a lot more sense than the traditional 12", 13", 16" set-up, where the intervals between the drums can make it difficult to create an even tonal progression. If you want to go down to the rumble of a 16" tom, why not try the more evenly spaced 10", 13" and 16"?

Another thing to consider is how the drums are mounted. For example, it's the current trend not to mount drums off the bass drum – which may look nice but does require more hardware – and while hanging floor toms were all the rage ten years ago there's been a recent return back to the good old-fashioned floor tom for probably just that reason.

As well as drum sizes, drum-shell depths have changed during the last ten years. Throughout the '80s, power toms prevailed, with shells almost as deep as they were wide. I can remember seeing a review for a kit with the old (what are now called 'standard-size') toms at the height of the power-tom era where the reviewer commented on what a brave move it was by the company in question. Well, within two years, things had turned around completely, with drum companies and endorsers singing the praises of shallower drums and their ability to 'speak' more quickly. 'Standard-size' drums *do* respond quicker; the laws of physics dictate it – the air has less distance to move before it meets the bottom head and gets it moving. This suits lighter playing situations or higher tunings, but power sizes will still work in louder environments, perhaps with double-ply heads fitted.

This same principle applies to snare drums. In the early '90s, the piccolo snare became popular because of its immediate, crisp response and sharp, cracking backbeat. This was probably a reaction to the thudding, reverb-soaked snares of the '80s, but it also serves to illustrate how shell depth affects a drum's response.

More recently, this idea of snare-drum shells getting smaller was taken in a different direction: instead of losing shell depth, a new breed of small-diameter snares has appeared. These have a similar response to a regular snare because of the similarity in depth, but they're much higher in pitch, enabling drummers to mimic the programmed sounds in today's music. The key is to choose a drum capable of producing the sound you want.

Let's take the drums and sounds mentioned earlier. If you play in a '70s-style rock band, a shallow or small-diameter snare drum isn't going to work as well as a deep wood or, possibly, metal drum no matter how low you try to tune it. This is where a selection of drums can help if you play several styles of music, but don't despair – you don't need a flightcase full of them; a deep wood drum and shallow metal drum will suffice, or vice versa, which with different tunings and dampening can see you through most situations.

While a drum's size and depth can affect its tone greatly, the material a drum is made from has a slightly lesser one, despite manufacturers' claims. If we were to believe all of the claims made in drum manufacturers' adverts – 'the new oak kit has more attack than the beech kit it supersedes, which had more overtones than the maple version, which had slightly more decay than the birch', and so on – we'd change kits every six months. In reality, while shell material plays a role, this can be over-emphasised, as can plies and reinforcement hoops. That's not to say that there's no difference between a budget wood-of-unknown-origin kit and a state-of-the-art maple kit – this much is obvious – but, if given a selection of high-end drums fitted with the same new heads and well tuned and mounted on similar suspension mounts, I believe in a blindfold test a lot of us would find it difficult to determine the different makes, let alone shell material or construction!

Cymbal Selection

The basis for most cymbal set-ups is the hi-hat, a ride cymbal and a crash, and you should really be able to say pretty much most of what you want to say using these three cymbals alone. (Incidentally, if you've never tried using that set-up, it really is worth giving it a go – using a stripped-down four-piece kit can actually feel kind of liberating.) Additional cymbals you might add would be another crash to complement the first, then maybe an effects cymbal such as a splash or china cymbal. About ten years ago, using another closed pair of hi-hats (X-hats) on the opposite side of the kit became popular. Dave Weckl (the pioneer of that approach) and many other drummers use them, as they enable you to play your left foot on the hi-hat while maintaining a closed-hi-hat sound, and unlike 'normal' hi-hats, in the regular position they allow access to the rest of the kit with the left hand. Dave Weckl stacks cymbals on top of each other (an 18" crash with a 14" china on top) for a raw, trashy sound, but probably the most outrageous purveyor of this approach is Terry Bozzio, who uses over 50 cymbals in his recent set-up.

Aside from types of cymbals, there is weight and durability to consider. If you play heavily, you'll need heavier cymbals, but if played and mounted correctly most cymbals should stand the test of time.

Firstly, always make sure that the cymbal isn't coming into contact with the stand, it should be mounted on some kind of sleeve. If it's not, the effect of metal on metal will 'keyhole' the cymbal in the centre. Also, avoid clamping down cymbals, even hi-hats – they should be allowed to move freely, as any resistance has to be absorbed by the cymbal. When hitting the cymbal, try hitting across it as opposed to into it. If you feel you need to use heavier cymbals, avoid extremes; I've seen drummers using heavy ride cymbals as crashes and they don't seem to be able to take the punishment. A more flexible cymbal of a similar size might be more appropriate.

When choosing ride cymbals, try to find a cymbal that has some crashing possibilities. You could even take a crash cymbal along to see if they blend together. Having a 'crashable' ride offers more flexibility than a cymbal that just goes *ping* or *clang*, as it will enable you to play it using the shoulder of the stick for a broad wash to match splashy open-hi-hat sounds, and it will also enable you to play accents within jazz time on the same cymbal, as opposed to having to crash everything on the crash cymbal.

The wash and spread of a riveted cymbal can be a really musical sound and makes a wonderful addition to a cymbal set-up. I have a few cymbals that I've been brave enough to drill and rivet with no fatalities in the cracking department. Incidentally, if you're going to try this, be sure to punch the mark first in order to avoid the bit slipping all over the cymbal. And use a sharp bit, supporting the cymbal on a piece of wood. This isn't for the faint-hearted, as there's a lot at stake. A less stressful alternative is a piece of plug chain – not quite as cool, but it offers you the option of turning your ride into a riveted cymbal mid-gig! Simply loop the end and drape it over the appropriate cymbal.

Electronics

'I react to sounds from electronics as I do to fireworks at Disneyland: I go, "Wow, that was great!" But fireworks at Disneyland are not anything like seeing a meteor explode – hearing a real snare drum and the beauty of the drum'. *Jeff Porcaro*

If this book had been written 15–20 years ago, it would probably have been called *100 Tips For Electronic Drummers*. Electronic kits were everywhere in the '80s and, led by Simmons, almost every major drum manufacturer dabbled in their own versions. Why were electronic kits so successful? I guess the flexibility in terms of available sounds was the main selling point. That and the fact that they can be turned down was – and still is – another one, especially for the practising drummer. Eventually, of course, the bubble burst, with Simmons over-investing in its groundbreaking SDX, which had more features than most drummers required – or could afford.

At around this time, producers began to move away from the dead, processed sound used throughout the '70s, and natural-sounding, open-tuned kits became the norm. Recent years, however, have seen a resurgence in electronic kits, with the invention of mesh heads that feel more like real drums. Technology has moved on as well, with the kits now residing in a virtual world where you're able to change rooms, heads, dampening and so on. Studio players are carrying these kits as part of their arsenal: they enable engineers to get good sounds quickly, and if the MIDI signal is recorded, you can change sounds completely in the mix.

Since the advent of electronic kits, one aspect that has remained popular throughout is triggering. This works in the same way as a pad triggers the sound from the module, only now it's triggered by a 'bug' mounted on the drum. This allows either the acoustic sound of the drum or the triggered sound – or a combination of both – to be used. This is often used by touring drummers, who use triggers to fire off sounds taken from the band's albums.

8 IN THE STUDIO

Entering a studio for the first time can be an exciting yet intimidating experience. The chances are that the studio time is being paid for by either the artist, the record company, the producer or maybe your own band, so from the word go the pressure is on to get good results as quickly as possible. This doesn't relate only to how quickly you can record your tracks, although that is obviously an issue, but if it's a session you'll have to take into account your ability to learn songs and adapt to changes.

Aside from your drumming skills there's another attribute that it's important to take with you to the studio: communication skills. This can range from being able to talk to the engineer on his own level ('the bass drum sound kind of woolly in the low mids' as opposed to 'that sounds awful') to understanding producers and songwriters ('I think the vibe should be more purple', or 'Stay tight with the click but keep it feeling loose!'). In this chapter, I'm going to look at all of these topics to help make your next visit to the studio a more rewarding experience.

I've always enjoyed the recording process, and from the beginning I've always asked questions about any part of the process I didn't understand. Although I don't think you need to be a studio engineer to get good results in the studio, understanding how things work will definitely help. What's more, engineers and producers are normally more than happy to share their insights and I've learned new ideas on things like microphone placement and signal processing as well as tuning and drum selection at just about every session I've done.

Be Prepared

In the studio, it's not only your drumming that's under the microscope; your drums will be listened to more closely than in most live situations, and any rattles, noisy bass-drum pedals or tuning discrepancies will soon be discovered. Dismantling a fully miked kit to tighten a screw in a bass-drum spur or floor-tom stand isn't a great help to the creative process, so it's a good idea to try to have your kit as studio-ready as possible.

The same applies to drum heads: old heads will sound lifeless and struggle to hold their tunings, so try replacing the relevant heads the day before the session (unless of course you're going for the old-school funk thing!), as opposed to when you arrive – there's usually plenty of other stuff to worry about.

Take as much equipment as you think you could possibly need. I like to carry at least two snares as well as a good selection of cymbals and a few shakers, tambourines and so on. A different snare can change the sound of the whole kit, and most producers like to come out and listen to the various sounds available. Even with only two snares, you'll probably find that one suits a particular track better than another.

'I feel like grooving more when the drums I'm playing have something cock-eyed about them. I find it disconcerting to play on a great-sounding studio kit.' *Jim Keltner*

Always ask where to set up your kit first, as there is generally a part of the room that the engineer knows sounds good for drums, but also be prepared for the times when this doesn't work. I once set up in the huge live room of an up-market studio yet ended up recording in a store cupboard to get a tighter sound!

'Some engineers might be very good, but they might be very set in their ways and think, "This is the only way I get drum sound." There are certain engineers I work for who even have snare drums: "This is my snare drum." Some of the drums may sound great, and there may be something special about them, but there's always the stick size and who's hitting it. You may use the same mic, with the same EQ, have your same level, record in the same room, and still it's going to sound different.' *Jeff Porcaro*

Miking Up

Once the kit's set up and tuned, it's time for the mics to be put in place. At this point, depending on the situation, you can do one of several things: get a cup of tea, check out the engineer's mic choice and placement or have a chat with the producer or songwriter about how they see the session going – or, if you're lucky, all three! Most contemporary music situations involve miking all of the individual drums (unless it's a jazz or acoustic-style session, which might use just overheads and bass-drum mics), with the reflective sound being captured by separate room mics that can be 'dialled' when required.

How Many Mics?

There seem to be two schools of thought regarding the number of mics it takes to get a good drum sound. One approach is the more natural, ambient-miked approach. This can be heard on jazz recordings and, in fact, most recordings up until the '70s, when multitracking became the norm. Until then, the drums were often captured on a single mic. In fact, I recall a great story where, at one of the top studios of its time, the engineers would walk around the live room as the band played and drop a coin on the floor at points where it sounded best. Where the coins were left, mics would be put up and blended together, giving the natural sound heard on so many old recordings.

These days, more control of the various elements of the kit is needed as sounds jostle for their places in fuller, more extreme-sounding mixes. Let's take a look at some of the other minimal mic set-ups.

Two mics mono. This arrangement uses just a bass-drum mic and an overhead. It's fine for capturing a basic sound and was probably the mic set-up of choice until stereo arrived

Three mics. This kit uses John Bonham's three-mic set-up. The two overheads – one directly over the snare, the other pointing at the floor tom – can be panned hard left and right for implied stereo

Three mics. This kit uses a jazz/ambient mic set-up, creating a very natural sound with good stereo imaging

Four mics. This four-mic set-up uses a configuration shown to me by Billy Ward. The bass drum and snare are close-miked while the overheads are placed low down, with one between the snare, hi-hats and rack tom and the other behind the floor tom. Both mics should be an identical distance away from the snare. This is best suited to four-piece set-ups and gives a full, natural sound

If more than four mics are used, the chances are that the toms will be individually miked, followed by hi-hats, overheads and finally room mics.

Mic Placement

When close miking, most drums are miked from the top, apart from the bass drum, of course (although occasionally mics are used on both tops and bottoms of snares and toms). This can help add to the sizzle of the snares or the liveliness of the toms.

The bass drum is usually miked from inside through a hole in the front head, providing isolation from the rest of the kit and helping to add more beater attack. If, however, the drum has a full front head, it is possible to mic from the outside, where a mic on the batter head pointing at the point of beater impact should give a reasonable balance of tone and attack.

Hi-hats are usually miked separately and from above to pick up the stick definition, often pointing away from the rest of the kit for more isolation. Miking

hi-hats from the side is usually avoided, as the mic can pick up the wind noise as the cymbals are closed.

The remaining cymbals are usually picked up with two overhead mics in stereo placed above the kit, but these can also be used to capture the whole of the kit as long as the cymbals aren't overplayed.

In larger recording situations, room mics are also added to capture the ambient sound in the room. These mics, usually consisting of one or more stereo pairs, can negate the need for processed ambience or reverb to be added and create a much more natural sound than most reverb units.

Snare And Toms

A good general rule of thumb is to place snare and tom mics three fingers' distance from the hoop (to reduce rim overtones) and pointing at the centre of the drum to pick up stick attack. If you play cross-stick during the song, pointing the mic at the point where the stick hits the rim can help bring out the click. (Incidentally, when playing a cross-stick sound, try turning the stick around for a fatter sound.) Miking the bottom of the snare will enable the sound of the snares to be blended in with the attack of the top head, but one of the mics may well need its phase reversing (see below). Try pointing the snare mic away from the hi-hats, as most dynamic mics pick up very little of what goes on behind them and, as you'll discover, hi-hats tend to bleed all over the snare-drum track. This means that, if you want to add some reverb to a snare track splattered with hi-hats, it will also go on the hi-hats themselves, creating a washy sound lacking in definition.

Bass Drums

If you want more attack in your bass-drum sound, place the mic inside the drum, pointing at the point where the beater hits the head. Try to avoid placing the mic directly behind the point where the beater hits, as the SPL (Sound Pressure Levels) could damage the mic – if you've ever held your hand in the centre of the front head of a bass drum when it's being played, you'll know what I mean. To capture more of the resonance inside

the drum, point the mic to the side or move it nearer the front head. If you use a closed front head, placing a mic in front of the drum can work (this can also reduce punch, however, so you could try miking the batter head with the mic again pointing at the point of beater contact). This mic will also contain a lot of snare, so be careful with extreme EQ as it will affect your snare drum sound too. Again, as with the snare, two mics are often used on the bass drum and blended together, although phasing can be an issue here.

Overheads

Overhead mics are usually placed directly above the kit and panned hard left and right, although they can also be placed in front of or behind the kit, or even on either side of the drummer's head to give a representation of what the drummer hears. One of the most common overhead placements is *coincident-pair miking*. Here the mics are positioned close together in a V-shape, with each pointing at the opposite side of the kit. This gives a natural stereo image without incurring phase problems as all sounds reach each mic at the same time.

Coincident Pair

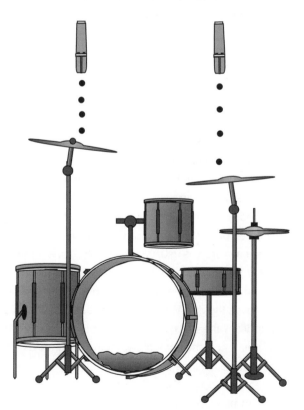

Spaced Pair

The other commonly used overhead placement is *spaced-pair miking*. This gives a wider stereo image than coincident-pair miking, but phasing issues can again occur as different sounds reach the different mics at different times.

Once the kit's miked and some drums have been recorded to tape, it can be a surprise when you go back into the control room and, as the engineer brings up the different faders, you discover that the bass-drum mic also has lots of snare drum in it and the snare-drum mic has picked up lots of hi-hat, and so on. It's important to appreciate that a microphone hears everything that's going on in that area of the drum kit, so, for example, the snare-drum mic will pick up predominantly snare drum, but hi-hats will be a close second followed by tom 1 and maybe some cymbals. This means that any processing done to the snare drum will also affect the other sounds captured by that mic. Therefore, if you want to add reverb or perhaps extreme EQ to the snare, this will also be heard on the hi-hats.

With this in mind, mic placement can really shape the overall drum sound. I recall seeing a drum kit set up in the next studio from where I was recording and the producer had taped cardboard around the mics to screen off other sounds. Unfortunately, while this approach might seem logical, microphones work in particular ways and have specific areas or patterns around them that pick up sound. If these are blocked, the response of the mic is greatly affected.

One of the ways in which these patterns can be affected in a positive way is if more bottom-end or low frequencies are required. Here, bringing the mic closer to the drum – maybe just an inch or two – introduces what's called the *proximity effect*, where the closer the mic is to the sound source, the more low frequencies it picks up.

Microphone Types

Microphones can be differentiated by how they operate. They basically fall into two types:

- **Dynamic mics** (also known as moving-coil mics) work like speakers, only in reverse. SPLs (Sound Pressure Levels) move a diaphragm that's connected to a coil whose movement in relation to a magnet creates a signal which is amplified by the mic pre-amp in the desk. Dynamic mics are ideal for use on drum kits because not only are they able to withstand high SPLs but they are capable of taking some serious abuse – which is particularly handy when dealing with a less-than-accurate drummer! The frequency response of the mics is also good, although not as good as that of condenser mics. Dynamic mics are usually used on snare drums, toms and bass drums.

- **Condenser mics** require 48V phantom power, sent to the mic via the cable. This is usually supplied from the desk, sometimes on individual channels, sometimes on banks and often – as on budget desks – on a single switch. It's good practice to avoid plugging in any mic into even a muted channel with the phantom power switched on, as this can create potentially disastrous noises. Also, always remember to power down, allowing a few seconds for residual current to dissipate before plugging in your mic. The power supplied is used by a small amplifier inside the mic which increases the voltage of the signal created by the movement of a diaphragm. Condenser mics are usually used on cymbals, toms and, occasionally, the underside or even the top of the snare.

Phasing

Phasing is caused when one signal cancels out another, creating a thin, hollow sound. This can usually be rectified by either physically moving one of the mics or switching the polarity of the mic. This can be done either by using the polarity-switching facilities on the desk or mic or by using a lead with the appropriate wires reversed.

One of the best ways to avoid phase-cancellation problems is to use as few mics as possible for your recording. The correct placement of the mics, as well as the choice of mic, should mean that a good drum sound can be achieved by using as few as three, four or five mics.

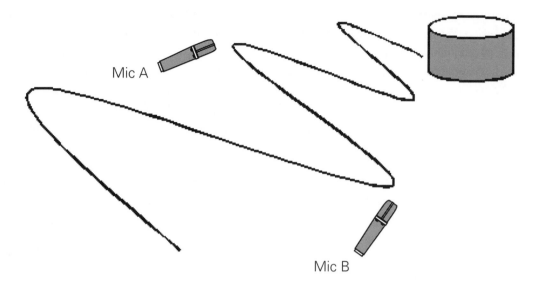

Mic A

Mic B

Mics A and B are picking up the signal 180° out of phase

As mentioned earlier, the more mics used, the more phasing problems can occur, but it also gives you more control over the elements of the kit. On the Tool album *Lateralus*, drummer Daney Carey used Neumann U87s on the tops and bottoms of all of the toms – that's £3,500 worth of mic on each drum! Yes, it sounds fantastic, but if you hear Billy Ward's sublime *Two Hands Clapping* CD, most of it is recorded with about five mics and it too sounds wonderful, so don't feel that your sound relies on a lot of mics; a few well-placed mics can give a truer representation of your kit.

'It cracks me up how many engineers never walk out into the room to hear what your instrument sounds like. They stay in the control room: "Snare drum doesn't sound good, man."' *Jeff Porcaro*

Recommended Mics

As we know, there are two types of mic commonly used, but which do we use to capture the different elements of the kit? Here's a list of some of some of the most popular choices.

Bass Drum Mics
- AKG D-12 or D-112
- Sennheiser MD-421
- Beyer M-88
- Shure Beta 52

- Shure SM91 Electro Voice RE-20

Snare Drum Mics
- Shure SM57
- Shure Beta 57
- Audix D1
- Electro-Voice N/D 308

Tom Mics
- Shure SM57/SM98/Beta 56
- AKG C408/C418
- Electro-Voice N/D 308
- Audix D2
- Neumann U-87
- Sennheiser MD-409/MD-421/MD-504

Hi-Hat Mics
- Shure SM84
- AKG 460
- Neumann KM-184
- Audio-Technica 4031/4051
- Audix SCX-1

Overhead Mics
- Rode NT1/NT2
- AKG 414
- Audio Technica 4050/4033
- Neumann TLM-193

It's good to know the model names of several mics, especially those that have worked for you in the past. When the situation allows, discuss mic selection and placement with the engineer. Tell him what works for you, but always be prepared to learn a new placement or use different mics – the more you know, the better.

Getting A Sound

After the drums are miked, the signal arrives at the mixing desk. This is where the sounds are processed and shaped to work within the music. There are essentially two types of desk: analogue and digital. An analogue desk generally requires other outboard equipment, such as reverb units and so on, and also requires 'hands-on mixing', where sounds are manipulated by hand as a mix is put together. A digital desk, on the other hand, often contains built-in processing equipment, and it can also be 'sync'd' to other equipment, thus allowing automated mixing. This is where the controls remember where they should move to within a mix and move themselves – kind of spooky when seen for the first time!

One of the most important elements of a desk is the pre-amp. This is often what makes the difference between large commercial desks and budget desks. Cheaper pre-amps simply aren't able to handle the high SPLs of kick and snare drums or the speed at which they appear. This is part of what you're paying for at bigger studios and why the drums sounds recorded therer often sound thicker, fatter and warmer.

The next thing to shape the drum sound is equalisation, or EQ. We've all messed around with the EQs on home stereos, although these are usually graphic EQs, which means that there are selected frequencies that can be increased or decreased. On mixing desks, high and low EQs work in this way, usually boosting or reducing all frequencies above or below the specified amount, and these are called *shelving EQs*. The mid range, however, is different; here a frequency can be selected and then adjusted by a *parametric EQ*. Most larger desks have hi-mid and lo-mid parametric EQs, offering lots of control and enabling you to turn a regular snare drum into a piccolo and vice versa.

A professional desk can be an intimidating-looking piece of equipment, more like the flight deck of an aeroplane than a piece of musical equipment, so on the next page you'll find a diagram of a smaller, but essentially similar, channel strip (of which there can be anything from 16 up to 48 on a desk) and a brief explanation of what the different components do.

Noise Gates

If you've ever been in the studio and, on hearing the mix, realised that some of what you played has gone missing, this is probably the result of over-gating (and possibly an unsympathetic engineer/producer!). A noise gate is used to close down a channel when the signal falls beyond certain point. As mentioned earlier, if you open any given mic on a kit, you'll hear all sorts of other sounds as well as the sound it's intended to pick up the most. Sometimes it can be necessary to eliminate these other sounds, leaving just the sound you want, but in reality this is often easier said than done.

Take the snare drum, for example. If we start to gate, the first things to go might be the cymbals, then the toms furthest away, and then, maybe, the bass drum. However, in order to eliminate the hi-hat and tom 1, the gate has to be closed so much that all of the ghost notes played on the snare are lost as well, leaving just the loudest hits on the snare. This can then be EQ'd without affecting the other sounds. Once this is blended in with the rest of the drum track, on which all of these other sounds can still be heard, it can still sound quite natural, but if gates are used elsewhere things can start to be lost, giving a rather unnatural sound.

As well as in those situations where EQing is affecting other sounds, gating can be useful if numerous open-tom mics are muddying a mix with their constant rumbling and ringing, or maybe there's noise from the guitarist's amp spilling over into the open mics. Gates can also be used to clean up a bass-drum or even, sometimes, a snare-drum track, leaving only a clean signal. A lot of pop and rock records use this kind of approach, and although it would sound odd if you were to hear just the kick and snare on their own, when the room mics are added it can be particularly effective.

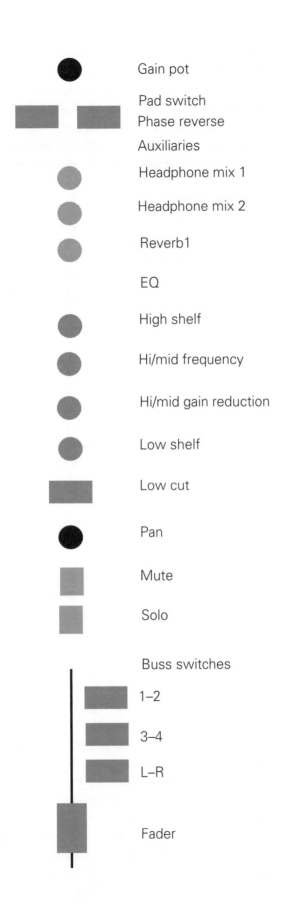

Gain pot

Pad switch
Phase reverse

Auxiliaries

Headphone mix 1

Headphone mix 2

Reverb1

EQ

High shelf

Hi/mid frequency

Hi/mid gain reduction

Low shelf

Low cut

Pan

Mute

Solo

Buss switches

1–2

3–4

L–R

Fader

The Channel Strip

The signal arrives at the desk on either a jack or XLR cable. At this point the gain pot is used to bring the signal to 0Db. This sometimes requires the use of the pad switch for signals that are too 'hot'. Phase can be reversed here as well.

Next up are the auxiliaries, which can be used as monitor or effects sends. Below that is the EQ. Here we're showing a simple three-band EQ with parametric mid range. The hi and low are set to a specific frequency, typically 10K and 80Hz respectively. Parametric mid-range requires two pots, with one pot selecting the frequency to be affected while the other increases or reduces it. On this mocked-up mixer there is also the option of a low shelf switch that can be used to remove unwanted low-end rumbles below a specified frequency.

Then we have pan, mute and solo. These are fairly self-explanatory with the pan pot used to place the signal anywhere between hard left and hard right in the stereo spectrum. The mute switch, when depressed, will take that particular channel out of the main mix. Solo, when depressed, will cut all of the other channels, leaving just the selected channel – good for auditioning sounds.

Next down is the fader. This should be set around unity (0dB on the fader) if the gain structure is set correctly. Next to that are the buss switches. In this case the desk is a four-buss desk, so if the 1-2 button is depressed this channel will be sent to sub-outs 1 and 2. If, however, the pan is set hard left, the signal will be sent to sub-out 1, and if set hard right to sub-out 2. This enables you group several sounds – toms, for example – to a stereo output, which is useful if you have limited tracks on which to record.

The L-R button simply brings this channel into the main mix.

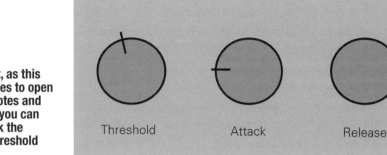

Threshold   Attack   Release

The threshold is very important, as this decides how much signal it takes to open the gate. This is where ghost notes and other subtleties can get lost. If you can hear this happening, simply ask the engineer if he can adjust the threshold

How It Works

A gate has three main controls: Attack, Release and Threshold. The Attack decides how quickly the gate opens after it's triggered (for drums, this should be as quick as possible so as not to clip the first part of the signal). The Release time decides how soon the gate closes. Deciding factors here could be how much room sound you want to allow through or how soon you want the unwanted sounds to appear.

When And Where?

In terms of at what stage of the recording it should be done, like most forms of processing it's best left until mixing because, once a signal is gated to tape, it's gone forever. As for situations that require gating, we discussed a few earlier, but other examples might be when the ambience of the room is doing nothing for the sound and you'd rather use a digital reverb. This might be the case in budget studios with eggboxes (which are essentially useless, by the way) on the walls, as opposed to a £1,000-a-day studio where you're paying for the ambience, not to mention the £10,000 worth of mics to capture it. In less glamourous situations, you may have to deal with a horrible-sounding room, in which case try miking close (including the cymbals) to eliminate as much of the room sound as possible.

Another gating idea used by Simon Phillips is to gate the reverb send. In other words, a dry, untouched snare is left in mix but the snare signal is sent to an auxiliary that is gated. This means that the only thing to get the reverb is the gated signal, so none of the hi-hat spill gets affected.

Compressors

Another invaluable piece of studio technology is the compressor, and the chances are that any piece of recorded music you hear has passed through one at some stage. When used on drums, compressors can make the sound punchier and more aggressive, bringing the recorded signal closer to the attack heard when sitting behind the kit. They work via a similar principle to noise gates and include similar features, such as Threshold, Attack and Release. As on the noise gate, the Threshold level decides at which point the compressor begins to work, but this time any signal beyond this point is reduced by a set amount (determined by adjusting the Ratio). This reduction of the peaks enables the whole signal to be run louder, hence the term *compression*. You could view it as more signal being squashed into the same space. The ratio decides how much compression is applied, so if a ratio of 2:1 is set with a threshold of 0dB and at some point the drummer slams the snare and creates a +4dB spike, the compressor will reduce it to +2dB.

This ratio can be set to more extreme settings for other reasons. For example, if it's set at 10:1 or more, it's basically working as what is known as a *limiter*. At this ratio, the signal will be unable to pass the threshold at all, allowing you to record without any spikes overloading the input of the recorder – or saving speakers in a live situation.

Attack, Release And Knees

The Attack and Release features work in the same way as the noise gate, with the Attack deciding how quickly the compression kicks in. For drums, obviously, the

Attack time must be quick. The Release time, which determines how quickly the compression lets up, must also be quick for drums, but other instruments, such as bass, may require a slower Release time. This principle of compressing all signals above the threshold by the amount decided by the ratio is known as *hard-knee compression*. Nowadays, a lot of compressors have the option of *soft-knee compression*, a more musical-sounding compression that works by compressing signals close to the threshold at a lower ratio.

When And Where?
Compression is usually done at the mixing stage, but compressed sounds can also be recorded. This means that the signal can be recorded 'hotter' (or louder), without distortion, so that when the same sound is compressed later there is less noise to compress.

The snare and bass drum are probably the first two elements of the kit to address, and as the peaks are removed it can make them sound more consistent. Toms can also be treated, but beware because the increase in level can cause the spill and sympathetic ring inherent in close-miked toms to get louder (unless gates are also being used). Cymbals/overheads can also be compressed, possibly with a slightly slower release time to create a smoother sound. If you're tracking in a nice-sounding room, compressing the room mics can add more air to the sound.

Reverb
The chances are that at some point you've set up your drums in a large hall and probably been inspired by the huge, ambient sound coming back at you. Unfortunately, most budget studios don't boast live rooms of this size, so it's necessary to approximate the effect by using digital reverb. This comes in the form of a processor designed specifically to imitate the character of different types of rooms and reverbs, from hall and cathedral to spring and plate. These effects are added by sending the dry (unaffected) signal to the processor via the auxiliary sends. The effect comes back either on the effect returns or, for more control, on their own stereo channel (the latter allowing the signal to be EQ'd to suit the track, which can be useful as naturally occurring reverb is rarely as bright as the initial sound). This is

then blended to the dry drums, with the resulting combination referred to as the *wet signal*.

When And Where?
Reverb is usually added during the mixing stage (and sometimes during monitoring, for a more inspiring sound), as opposed to tracking. Again, if the drums are recorded to tape with the effect, there's no turning back. If you were to listen to a kit played in a large room, you'd hear the ambience on everything, but if using the digital equivalent gives you the luxury of being able to apply it to any part you want. This would usually begin with the snare, which can sometimes be the only drum to receive reverb (it can make the whole kit sound bigger). Next might be the toms, which can receive the same reverb or less – maybe about half the amount – to make the kit sound like it's been recorded in the same room. The remaining elements – bass drum, hi-hats and overheads – are usually best left dry. In fact, the hi-hats are one part of the kit that really should avoid reverb treatment.

If we go back to the hall we started in, every time a drum is hit there's a slight delay before we hear the reflected sound. This is called *pre-delay*, which helps to give a drum sound a sense of place. On most reverb units, this setting can be adjusted and even calculated to last for a specified length, such as a 16th note. This can be really useful in cleaning up a track that requires a lot of reverb.

The Big Picture
Out of all of the instruments, the drum kit has probably had more pages of recording magazines dedicated to it than any other. It's a notoriously difficult instrument to capture because there are so many elements covering such a wide range of frequencies and dynamics, and even when good individual sounds have been achieved, it's still possible for them to be balanced incorrectly, losing the impression that it's a single entity.

When trying to capture the natural sound of a kit, I find that two things help me. Firstly, I mix the kit as though I'm sitting behind it. I find it easier to visualise the kit in front of me and relate the sounds to the mental picture I have. For example, I keep the kick and snare dead centre, pan the four toms in the 3, 1, 11 and 9 o'clock positions, with the overheads panned hard left and right. This tends to give a fairly natural representation of how my kit is set up.

The other important ingredient in getting a natural sound is to compare the recorded sound with the sound in the room. Don't forget that this is where your sound begins, and no amount of processing is going to make a bad-sounding recording great.

If, however, you're trying to achieve a very processed sound where the kit sounds larger then life, then there really are no limits. I've done sessions where the producer has had me record without toms for better separation. You could also look at gating or triggering, where thicker sounds are added to the acoustic sounds. This approach is often used by rock drummers to stand up to walls of distorted guitar.

The Control Room

When you first go back into the control room after recording a take, don't expect to hear a finished product. The chances are that the track will be flat, with little or no EQ, and as I mentioned earlier, when you hear the component parts of the kit individually it can sound somewhat different from your usual impression of your kit. There may well be no processing, in terms of reverb or compression, and this can make the kit sound small and lacking in power. The opposite of this is the engineer who floods everything in reverb and turns the monitors up to 11. In these situations, it's difficult to hear whether your kit is sounding right, and although you may feel awkward, ask to listen to individual elements of your kit dry just to be sure.

Communication

There can be a lot at stake when you go into the studio. You're trying to capture the perfect piece of playing to complement the music while someone is spending money. Tensions can run high when things aren't going well, and comments like 'My bass drum sounds like shit' aren't going to help. When communicating with the engineer, try to let him know what you're hearing. If you don't know what it is in terms of EQ ('Can you pull out 3 or 4dB at about 500Hz?'), then say something like, 'The bass drums sounds woolly in the low mids.'

Most producers and engineers like to come into the room and hear the kit acoustically. What they don't need is for you to stomp on your bass-drum pedal as they're adjusting the mic placement inside the drum!

No Practising!

There's a well-known jingles studio in London's West End that used to have a sign in the drum booth saying, 'No Practising'. Although I think it was intended as a joke, there's an element of truth in the saying, as there's nothing more annoying than a drummer – or anyone else, for that matter – making a noise while other players are discussing parts or tuning up. In the studio, everything you play is in everyone's headphone mix as well as the studio monitors, so if you're happy with your sound, set-up and drum part, try to play only when you need to and save it for the take. If you need some time to work on a part, ask the engineer to give you a few minutes and he can turn the monitors down and wait until you're ready.

Control Freak

'When I listen back to stuff I'm currently working on, sometimes they change things in the mix or whatever and I'm like, "Why did they make it sound like that?". Then you have to think that they've been hired to do it. I don't question it as much as I used to. I take it in my stride now.'
Vinnie Colaiuta

Recording electric guitar is relatively simple: put a dynamic mic in front of the amp and turn up the fader. Drums, however, are far more complicated. There are a lot more elements to process and balance, and in the wrong hands what might have been a great take can end up sounding nothing like the sound you wanted. In those situations where you have a say in the finished sound – perhaps a band demo, for instance – it can be a good idea to help the engineer understand the kind of sound you're after. This can be difficult to put into words, so bringing along a few CDs can help. As your experience in the studio increases, you'll be able to talk to the engineer on his own level as well as offer your own suggestions on how to achieve the best results.

9 PLAYING LIVE

For some people, playing live is the most enjoyable part of playing an instrument, as in a live situation you get an immediate response to your playing, unlike playing in the studio. I've played literally thousands of gigs in the UK, Scandinavia, Europe, Russia and the USA, and whether I'm playing to 30,000 people or 30, the same principles apply.

Set-Up

For a lot of gigs, the drummer is expected to set up on the ubiquitous drum riser. This can take a range of forms, from a sheet of plywood supported by beer crates to the roll-on/roll-off affairs used at festivals. After the novelty of using these wore off, I realised that it felt as though I was isolated and playing my own gig. Not only that, but risers make eye contact really difficult. Eye contact is so important on stage because, no matter how well rehearsed the set might be, there are always unforeseen situations to deal with. Try setting up so that you have good visibility, at least with the band member responsible for cues such as endings. I even reposition cymbals in order to see the necessary people

Another thing to consider as you set up is your proximity to amps. On smaller gigs, the chances are that guitar and bass amps won't be going through the PA, so they'll probably be fairly loud on stage. I recall Kinks drummer Bob Henrit saying how he always set up behind the line of the amps to save his ears. Given the volumes at which some guitarists like to play, that seems a sensible move!

On the subject of volume, beyond a certain point the drums will need to be amplified. For smaller gigs,

I carry my own monitor, into which I can directly plug my bass drum. It also has another input into which I can add another feed from the main desk for vocals. I find that on gigs where the drums aren't miked the first thing I miss is the bass drum, and the monitor adds just enough definition to the drum to help me out.

On most bigger gigs, the drums will usually go through the front-of-house desk. At this point your sound is usually in the hands of someone else, so it's a good idea if you can get someone else in the band to play your kit so that you're able to go out front to listen for tuning, balance, EQing, gating and processing. Watch out for the engineer who leaves everything set up from the previous drummer, including gates set up for someone else's dynamics. Beware also of the person who thinks that your drums should sound as though you're playing in a cathedral. This is often the same engineer, who, as howling feedback ensues halfway through the gig, is nowhere to be seen.

Monitoring

After seeing Dave Weckl on tour using his Yamaha O1V digital desk, I decided to take my own on the road and, like Dave, mix my own sound. Dave's reason for doing this is that he's spent years developing his balance and dynamics, so why put them in someone else's hands? My reason, although similar, was because I knew that the chances of finding the same processing equipment – not to mention mics – at every gig was slim, to say the least. The other advantage of the O1V is that the desk has 'total recall', giving you exactly the same set-up from the previous gig. With the mic packages aimed specifically at drummers, I think this sort of thing will become more commonplace over time.

Miking and processing your own sound is one thing, but how do you monitor it? On any gig, monitoring drums can be a problem. If you want to hear your drums as you play, they need to be pretty loud in the monitor, but this is a recipe for feedback. Toms are especially prone to it, but the bass drum and even the snare can end up feeding back, also. The answer is either gating the sound or in-ear monitoring. Most clubs use gates, but if you really want to hear the sound of your drums the only solution is in-ear monitoring. This can be difficult to integrate into a club monitor system, but if the system belongs to your band you could soon have CD-quality mixes and save your hearing (do beware of running them too loud, though).

Just to dispel a myth about in-ear systems, it's the wireless set-up that is expensive – the actual earphones (such as Shure's E1s) cost around £100, and as drummers we can easily use just the earphones plugged directly into a desk.

Once you're in a position where a monitor mix is available, whether using in-ears or not, the next to address is what to put in it. It's best to opt for as little as possible, because with too many sounds – and perhaps less-than-perfect monitors – the adjustments required throughout the gig can make it feel more like you're mixing a record than playing live. Personally, I like to start with the bass drum and vocals and then have the band play a tune, adding whatever sounds I'm missing. In-ear set-ups can require much more work as the earpieces tend to block out some of the natural sound of the kit and the on-stage sound, so you might need to begin with the whole of the kit.

Another reason for using in-ears is to monitor click tracks. When I joined Republica, the drummer was expected to monitor the click through the drum fill (monitor). This meant that the click was run pretty loud and bled into the drum mics, to be heard out front. Using in-ears means that no one needs hear the click, enabling the sequencer to be used much more discreetly.

Be Prepared

If you're lucky enough to gain some success as a drummer, the chances are that you'll eventually have your own drum tech setting up your drums, cleaning your cymbals and drinking your beer. However, most of the time it's up to you to check that your gear's in good working order as well as to carry the necessary spares to remedy any problems. I always carry a spare kick and snare head, hi-hat clutch, bass-drum spring and, of course, drum key.

Another essential is something on which to set up your drum kit. I remember doing a gig on a wooden floor with no mat while playing to a click (I wish I had that on video!), and needless to say it wasn't one of my better performances. Some companies make mats especially for that purpose, and of course these can also be marked with tape to show where stands and pedals should be placed for quicker setting up.

Get On, Get Off, Get Home

Apparently, this approach – 'the three Gs' – is attributed to a well-known tour manager in the '60s. For some people, however, going on stage isn't quite that easy, as nerves begin to eat into you away well before a gig. I'm fortunate in that, while I do feel a bit anxious before some gigs, especially if it's really important, I've never felt nervous to the point where I didn't want to go on. Yet I've seen people physically ill at the prospect of going on-stage. Unfortunately, I don't have any miracle cure for nerves, but just remember that the audience have come to see you play and that all you can do for them is play to the best of your ability on that day. Perhaps you'll make a mistake – I've been on stages where some show-stopping mistakes have been made – but at the end of the day, it's just music. No one's life is at risk. Just relax and enjoy having the best seat in the house.

10 PUTTING IT ALL TOGETHER

'I'm certainly not against good technique and articulate chops. I love hearing that sort of playing done well. I guess the thing is, though, since I can't do it as well as my favourites, I prefer to do it the simplest way I can.' Jim Keltner

As you begin to piece this material together, try to avoid the temptation of playing something inappropriate because you've just learned how to do it. I guess we've all been guilty of doing this at some point, but it's not really fair on the music. If the tune needs some simple drums, enjoy making the song work with very little – and there really is an art in that, as any of the great session drummers will tell you.

Also, try to keep things simple when you approach a tune for the first time. If you play a basic part that simply holds it all together, it gives you the opportunity to listen and decide what the tune really needs, as opposed to rushing in with 'funk beat 25'. This 'keep it simple and listen' approach can really work in situations where you're unsure of the tune. John Riley told me once that if he had to play a jazz tune he was unfamiliar with he'd play basic jazz time and count the bars in each of the sections so that, by the time the head had been played twice and the solos had begun, he knew the form. This is important if you're expected to solo over the tune later on.

'The only thing I think about for a drum fill is that it is right for a particular part of the song. I hate having to play a fill for a fill's sake, or just because you're at a turnaround or at the end of an eight-bar phrase.' Jim Keltner

Choose the time for your fill carefully. Think of it as your opportunity to prepare the listener for an impending change within the music. Or try a different approach – playing a fill but no crash on 1, for example,

or maybe an open hi-hat on the 'and' of 4 and closing it on 1, which can create the effect of pulling you into the next section.

Another idea that can work well if the next section drops in dynamics is to hit a loud flam on the snare on 1 and then drop down in volume, perhaps to a cross-stick on the snare. A similar approach is playing a flam on the snare or floor toms on the last 16th-note or eighth-note triplet of a measure but with no crash on 1. Or hitting a crash with no bass drum at the end of a phrase where the drums pull out can feel like the ground had a fallen away beneath you.

'Elvin Jones is way into the mental aspects of drumming. I remember asking him why sometimes I would play well and other times I would just suck. He called it "I thoughts". In other words, if you're playing and any sentence that starts with "I" comes into your head, like "I'm doing great", you're in trouble. Elvin told me that if you're thinking that way, you're not playing for the music. I'll never forget that.' Billy Ward

Be Yourself

'A lot of drummers think that as soon as they start playing they have to sound like themselves without realising that they don't yet have a self. I think it's more important to pick individual players from the past and try to play like them… I think the way I started sounding like myself was by learning all the great things they played and then making a kind of mental graph of what each player didn't do, and started to fill in the spaces they had left with my own playing.' *Tony Williams*

Learning from your favourite players is an important part of the learning process, and knowing other people's licks and grooves is nothing to be ashamed of. Obviously, if you try to base everything you play on someone else's style, you need to spend some more time being yourself, but understanding other drummers and how they play can be a great asset. Sometimes, if I'm trying to find the right feel for a specific tune, I find that trying to play like the drummer who defines that style – whether that's Elvin Jones or Gregg Bissonette – helps me to find the right part.

'I wouldn't call it stealing, but I've had people who've influenced me, and I'll like something and maybe use them. That's all part of the learning process. But if you start incorporating other people's things into your thing, you can lean on that too much, and that's almost like forging somebody's signature.' *Vinnie Colaiuta*

A Final Word

'The mark of a good drummer is how well you accompany people in all situations. For me, a good drummer is a drummer who can read, who can play in a country-and-western band, who can play behind a singer like Tony Bennett or Nancy Wilson, who can play brushes, who can play Latin music or who can play whatever they're asked to play.' *Tony Williams*

There's a lot information presented in this book, and some bits of it will be easier to assimilate than others. Firstly, don't get despondent when progress seems slow. Remember, Rome wasn't built in a day. Just try to enjoy your progress, slow as it may seem at times.

The other point I want to talk about is piecing all of this stuff together. After all, it's a good balance of all these various areas, as well other non-drum-related things such as punctuality and reliability, that we need to make us good, all-round drummers.

One way to make sure it's all coming together is to play music with other people. This may seem obvious, but I think it can be easy to overlook the importance of playing with others when locked in the practice room. You can keep a check on this in a couple of ways. The first and best is by playing with other people as often as possible. If, however, your job or location makes this difficult, try playing along to some music regularly. These are the best ways of seeing which areas of your playing need attention. Also, try playing something new once in a while. For example, play some jazz or go to a jazz jam if you're new to it. Or try for a different band, or maybe a show. It's amazing what working with different musicians in different situations will do for your playing.

Another important point is to try to play with people who are better than you. I've learned so much from these kinds of situations, and most musicians have been really helpful and supportive, offering advice and telling me what CDs to buy and so on.

It's also important to spend time listening to lots of different styles of music, not just your favourites. Listen to the drums parts and how they relate to a song as well the sound of the drums and how they fit in with the production. As an extra challenge, try to listen for the tuning, the cymbal choice and the room in which the drums were recorded.

Another thing that can really help inspire you is going to watch a good drummer play. It's great that these days we have DVDs and videos on which watch our favourite players, but you really can't beat seeing these people up close, watching them respond to and shaping the music.

'I think it's a fallacy that the harder you practise, the better you get. You only get better by playing. You could sit around in a room, in a basement, with a set of drums all day long and practise rudiments and try to develop speed, but until you start playing with a band you can't really learn technique, you can't learn taste, you can't learn how to play with a band and for a band.' *Buddy Rich*

Any Questions?

If you've any questions regarding anything in this book, feel free to drop me a line via my website, which can be found at www.peteriley.net